Your child from 5–11

YOUR CHILD
from
5 - 11

A PARENTS' HANDBOOK

JENNIE & LANCE LINDON

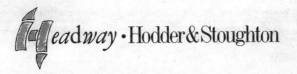
Headway · Hodder & Stoughton

To Peter and Annette;
close friends and fellow parents

British Library Cataloguing in Publication Data

Lindon, Jennie
  Your Child from 5–11. – (Positive
  Parenting Series)
  I. Title II. Lindon, Lance III. Series
  155.42

  ISBN 0-340-54750-2

First published 1993
Impression number   10 9 8 7 6 5 4 3 2
Year   1998 1997 1996 1995 1994

Typeset by Rowland Phototypesetting Limited, Bury St Edmunds, Suffolk.
Printed in Great Britain for Hodder & Stoughton Educational, a division of
Hodder Headline Plc, 338 Euston Road, London NW1 3BH by
Cox & Wyman Limited, Reading, Berks.

Positive Parenting

Positive Parenting is a series of handbooks primarily written for parents, in a clear, accessible style, giving practical information, sound advice and sources of specialist and general help. Based on the authors' extensive professional and personal experience, they cover a wide range of topics and provide an invaluable source of encouragement and information to all who are involved in child care in the home and in the community.

Other books in this series include:

Talking and your child by Clare Shaw – a guide outlining the details of how speech and language develops from birth to age 11 and how parents can help with the process.

Your child with special needs by Susan Kerr – a guide for the parents of the one-in-five children with special needs, giving families practical advice and emotional support, based on the shared experiences of other parents.

Whereas the authors of this series have offered ideas and practical suggestions in the light of their own experience and knowledge, only parents have the personal knowledge of their own family and children to enable them to make a sensible decision about what they will try and what could be best for them.

Contents

About the authors   ix

Acknowledgements   xi

1   **Parenting**   Being a parent. What only
    parents can do. Using the book.   1

2   **Helping children learn**   What parents can
    do. How do children learn? Helping your
    child to learn. Helping your child to study.
    Tests and exams.   5

3   **Change and your family**   Planning change.
    Family rules and change. Childrens
    responsibilities. Change and crisis. Family
    life/School life.   23

4   **Communication within the family**   Basic
    communication. Conversations and ideas.
    Conversations and problems.   43

5   **Growing up**   Teaching independence.
    Taking care of themselves. Growing up
    physically.   55

6   **Money matters**   Handling money. Fashion,
    clothes and money.   72

7   **Taking care – keeping safe**   Child care.
    Dangers to health. Teaching safe behaviour.
    On the move – letting your children go.   81

8   **Friends and friendship**   Friendship. Inviting
    friends round. Disputes between friends.
    Pressures from friends. Bullying.   99

9   **Doing things together**   Physical activities

and games. Sit-down games. Hobbies and
interests.   120

10 **Growing together** Conclusions: 133

   Resources People. Organisations.   137
   Index   143

About the authors

Jennie and Lance Lindon work as psychologists. Over the years they have worked with a wide range of people from social services and education, to business and commercial organisations. Jennie works as an independent trainer and consultant. Lance is a management development consultant with Sundridge Park Management Centre.

Just as importantly, they are also parents, with a son, aged eleven, and a daughter, aged nine. Becoming parents themselves added another dimension to their work with people who cared for and educated other people's children. They were impressed that many of the practical ideas they shared with adults in their business lives were equally useful in the task of bringing up children.

Acknowledgements

Our special thanks go to Annette Yates, who was the first person to suggest that we should write a book for the forgotten over-fives. We are grateful for her continuing ideas in conversations with Jennie. We also want to thank Maggie Harris who made very valuable comments on our almost final draft.

We have enjoyed many conversations with people who work with young children and their families. They felt, like us, that the practical books largely disappeared after the fifth birthday. We are grateful to the business executives who were honest enough to say that it would be less easy to apply our suggestions about communication in their work, but who were certainly going to use them at home with their children, and also to all our friends and acquaintances, with children ranging from babies to adults, who shared the satisfying and the totally infuriating parts of being a parent.

It would be very dishonest if we did not give our whole-hearted thanks to our children – Drew and Tanith – the most stringent testers of any of our practical ideas about parenting.

—

CHAPTER ONE

Parenting

Being a parent

As a parent, your responsibility is to run your family to the best of
your ability. This usually means juggling the different priorities and
the needs of all the individuals involved. Most of all, it comes down
to time and how to divide it up between the long list of things you
have to get done.

We believe that children are important and deserve your time,
attention and respect. We do not view them sentimentally as little
wisps of angel dust, but on the other hand, even in times of great
stress, we hold to the belief that they are not actually related to
the beast from forty thousand fathoms. In the main, children lie
somewhere in between. They are hard work, but they are worth it.

Your children deserve space to themselves and time from you.
The other adults in your life also require some of your attention. It
is not unreasonable, on the face of it, for you to have some time
to yourself, doing what you would like to do – just apparently
impossible.

There are many books about babies and toddlers and still a fair
number about life with older under-fives. This book, however, is
designed to help you and your family make the move into life with
the *over*-fives. Life does not generally get any easier with the five
to elevens; it does, however, take on a different form.

We offer suggestions, ideas and information to make the best of these 'different' years with your children. We are writing for fellow parents who care what happens to their children. We are certainly not recommending that you try to turn yourself into Supermum or Superdad. Part of being a parent is realising that your energy is finite, like your patience, although you do draw on reserves you never would have believed possible before you had children.

We have written this book primarily for parents. You may be a mother or a father; you may be a step-parent. We have used the word 'parent' in this book to cover any and all of you who are responsible for the parenting of children aged between five and eleven. However, if you are an adult responsible for children out-side the family, please don't put the book down. Many of the ideas could be relevant to workers in after-school clubs or holiday schemes and some may be helpful if you work voluntarily with groups like Cubs or Brownies.

We are also aware that some of you will have one child and some will have more. You may have daughters or sons. Consequently, we have rung the changes in this book between talking about 'your child' and 'your children' and we have made a single child some-times 'he' and sometimes 'she'. It will be obvious if we are making a point about girls rather than boys, or if we are talking about the situations that can arise with a family of several children.

What only parents can do

We don't see parenting as a job – who in their right mind would take it on? The hours are dreadful, the job description keeps chang-ing and you aren't allowed to resign. The task of parenting is prob-ably the most valuable work that adults do, yet it has ambivalent status in our society. There is no shortage of advice aimed at parents – some of it rather patronising – and equally, there is a readiness to blame parents as totally responsible if something goes wrong.

Some publications address parents largely on how they can support other people in their children's lives, such as teachers or doctors. Certainly, you do need to be able to collaborate with professionals who work with your children. However, our main interest lies in what parents can do and nobody else can, at least not in such a coherent way.

As a parent, you are uniquely placed to teach your children the skills of adulthood. You can help them grow towards independence in a more thorough way than anybody else. You are not just in charge of them for a year, like their primary school teacher; you can take your time and build up what your children need to understand.

The period from five to eleven years is an ideal time for teaching the beginning of true independence. Your children have both the interest and the developing capability. You have the opportunity to build on the life you had with them when they were younger. You also have a chance to grow with your children as you help them to develop independence.

We are sure that parts of this book will be a source of new ideas for every reader. Equally, there will be some parts that describe good things that you are doing already. Take the credit and congratulate yourself for doing well. Parents are often more ready to criticise themselves for what's gone wrong than to take the praise for success. Building on successes provides a firm basis for tackling those issues about which you feel less sure.

Using the book

This book will be most useful to you if you read it in the order that suits you best. The Contents will give you a rough idea of what we cover in each chapter, while the Index may help if you are looking for something in particular. Our only suggestion is that you at least take a look at Chapter 2 before moving on. How children learn is central to so many of the ways in which you can help them.

There simply wasn't the space in this book to include everything that we would have liked. For instance, we say very little about children's physical health. We have dealt with school mainly in terms of your relationship with teachers and helping your child to study. We have therefore given you leads for useful books and organisations, both within the different chapters and in the Resources at the back.

Only you can decide how you will use the ideas in this book. Your child is a unique individual, although he or she will share some things in common with you and with friends. In order to help, you have to be willing to stand back and look at your children as more than just extensions of yourself.

All parents have to resist setting themselves the impossible goal of being the 'perfect' parent. Nobody is. Doing well by your children is being prepared to start afresh each day or week and to keep trying. Good parenting is being prepared to think things over. It is also allowing for the fact that sometimes the most useful approach will be for you to change how *you* behave, rather than wishing that your *child* should act differently.

CHAPTER TWO

Helping children learn

What parents can do

Just because your children have entered the formal school years doesn't make you any less important. Of course, you will help as you can with their school work. However, you are better placed than anyone else to help your children to:

- Learn to take care of themselves in the widest sense.
- Have confidence in themselves as they are, and in their ability to develop further.
- Learn ways of coping and facing problems which will set them in good stead for the future.

To boost your confidence as a parent, do remember that your expertise is based on a long-term relationship that has already developed with your child. Other people will come and go. You provide your child's continuity.

Some professionals in all sorts of fields – doctors, teachers, social workers – occasionally make pronouncements about how parents are too emotionally involved with their children to make a balanced decision. The claim is sometimes that parents fail to see the big picture. Of course parents are emotionally involved with their children, and so they should be, and of course this will influence your judgement, because you will see your child at the centre of an issue. However, this does not make your way of looking at the situation wrong; it just makes it different. It is important that you work to understand the perspective of any professional who could help your child or your family. But remember, your task is to champion your children, accepting them warts and all.

How do children learn?

Your children will be learning at home as much as at school, although they may be learning different things. You will be able to help best if you can grasp *how* children learn as well as *what* they could be learning. Do bear in mind the following points.

Learning takes time

Learning something – especially if it is complex – is usually managed in bits. Linking these bits takes time and meanwhile children can get confused.

Suppose you want to teach your seven-year-old son to cook. You have been cooking for years; you may have forgotten what it was like not to know something simple, such as how high to put the gas. You have to tell and show him in digestible chunks of information, and shouldn't be surprised if he makes mistakes over things that seem obvious to you. They're not obvious to him; he hasn't learned that bit yet.

Learning needs concentration

To learn anything, children and adults have to attend. They have to focus for some length of time. The attention span of children aged between five and eleven gets longer but may be as short as five to ten minutes at the younger end. Children vary, of course, and you will notice that they may concentrate totally on some things that you wish they took less seriously – like computer games.

Five- to eleven-year-olds are learning to screen out some distractions. They may be able to get back to their activity from an interruption in a way that three- or four-year-olds would find impossible. However, even the best motivated children will be distracted by noisy classrooms or constant interruptions. Nine- and ten-year-olds can often persevere in their work for thirty to forty minutes, or longer, especially if you are a friendly and supporting presence. If your child has great difficulty concentrating, you may need to focus on helping him, by sitting down for short bursts and giving him a hand to see something through from start to finish.

Unless children attend, they won't be able to remember what you have told or shown them. The same will be true for their schoolwork. Children cannot summon up something from their memory that never made it there in the first place. Learning to concentrate is also about persistence – sticking at something, completing a piece of work, or memorising some information. This is hard work.

Different ways to learn

In order to learn effectively, we all need to do the following four things:

- Get on and do something or have some experience that provides information to work on.
- Think over what has happened and watch from time to time rather than be constantly in the thick of the action.
- Make some sense of the experience in order to be more ready in the future – a working theory about what is going on, what may work.
- Experiment, try something out based on the working theory.

Your children, like you, will have some favourite ways of approaching familiar and unfamiliar situations. Over time you will be getting to know how you can help your children to learn best, given their preferences. Does your son tend to think over something so much that he often does not get around actually to doing anything? Is your daughter so keen to get on with it that she is failing to learn obvious lessons of experience or good shortcuts? As an adult setting out to help, you also need to balance between sharing useful information, including your tried and tested short-cuts, and letting children find out for themselves.

Helping your child to learn

There are several ways that you can be a real help to your child.

Using everyday opportunities

Recall that children learn the knowledge and skills that they need a little at a time. So conversations and doing things together in the normal course of family life works very well. You can share ideas, opinions and information. Encourage your children to join in with your conversations and activities, and join in with theirs.

You can let them try things as you spend time together. Activities, which seem very ordinary to you, can be intriguing to them because it is their chance to look into the adult world. For example, five-to eleven-year-olds are often fascinated by banks. Take any oppor-tunities, as they arise, to show and explain and to give children practice in skills and ideas. Some things they will discover for them-selves; some things you will tell them. As they develop their own interests, they will tell you things you don't already know. Our own son, for instance, is considerably better informed about marine life, especially sharks, than either of us.

Taking everyday opportunities can be just as useful – or even better sometimes – than sitting down deliberately with your child for a work session. Keep alert to when your children are not in the mood to learn from you or when they have had enough for now. They may tell you this. They may, of course, just wander off, leaving you in mid-sentence.

You can help children sharpen up their skills of observation by playing spotting games. On journeys, even mundane ones to the shops, you can point out interesting things and chat about what you have noticed. Sometimes, of course, you and your children are happy in a companionable silence. We are not suggesting that you drown them in chat. The key is to give any child your full attention regularly. That is, not all the time. There are occasions when you have to concentrate on what you are doing or when you are tired. It is better to give your child ten or fifteen minutes of your undivided attention than to spend double this time while your mind is obviously fully occupied with something else.

Specific work times

These are in addition to and not instead of conversations with your children on a more casual basis. A particular 'Let's spend ten minutes on . . .' can be a good idea for several reasons:

- Children often enjoy doing some work.
- Many activities, like hearing your children read, especially in the early stages of learning, cannot be done properly whilst you are trying to do something else at the same time.
- You may want to help them understand something they find confusing – something which needs to be dealt with 'properly' rather than just as and when the situation arises. Taking opportunities as these arise is not working.

These 'sit-down' times with your child *may* be related to school matters, such as problems with sums, but not necessarily. It may be that you want a serious chat about a family issue, for example, 'You don't seem to be able to talk to grandpa'. There is more about talking over problems in Chapter 4.

Your encouragement

Most of us, children and adults alike, would welcome more compliments than we get. Your child will appreciate a genuine 'Well done' or 'You have improved so much'. Part of encouragement is being told how to do better in a way that does not make you feel put down. You can encourage your child with constructive comments if you follow these guidelines:

- Be accurate in what you tell your child. It doesn't help in the end to be told you are doing fine when you're not.
- Tell your child the useful details, like 'You're nearly always right when you tell the time now. It's the "quarter tos" that still catch you out, isn't it?' or 'I can see you are so much better at mixing cakes now. Just let me show you again how to crack an egg.'
- Keep an encouraging balance between what your child is doing well and what is going wrong – positive and negatives. Some children, like some adults, focus more on failures or near failures.
- You can be tentative in your suggestions so that your child does not feel daunted. You can try phrases like 'It might help if you tried . . .' or 'I found that this helped' rather than telling her to 'Do it this way.'
- You can remind your child of the progress he has already made. For example, writing his name is so easy now and he told you two months ago that he would never, ever be able to do it.

Watch out for interesting material

Children will find it more difficult to remember a topic that is presented in a boring way. Of course, having colourful books or using a video to enliven a subject does not remove all the hard work of remembering, but it does make it more likely that children's attention will be held – a crucial first step. You can help your children by encouraging them to learn from a wide range of different sources, including books, television programmes and increasingly magazines and newspapers. You can help them to make links between different sources on the same topic through chatting to them.

Seeking additional help

However much you want to, it is not always possible to help your child. You may be blocked by real problems of finding the time, or you may doubt your ability in certain areas. Some skills and areas of knowledge are best taught by specialists. For example, you may wish your children to have religious instruction. If you are a Christian family, this will probably mean sending them to Sunday School, or if you are a Muslim family, they may attend Quran classes.

On other occasions, you may be able and willing to help your child, but an unexpected pitfall creates emotional wear and tear on both of you. For example, if your child is really confused or very worked up about schoolwork, it is likely that you will suffer the full flood of upset and frustration that she has managed to hold back in the classroom. This can be very heavy-going on both of you. Eventually you will come through this together, but it will often need all your reserves of patience and persistence. Sometimes, the emotional price is too high and you need to find someone else who can help.

In the case of schoolwork, it may be that your expectations, or those of your child, are too high and you are worrying unnecessarily – check with the teacher. However, it may be that your child does need additional help. Can another teacher that your child likes at school help? Could you afford a private tutor on Saturday mornings? Could another family member, one step away from the situation, assist?

If your child is identified as having a learning difficulty like dyslexia, then you do need specialist input. Your task then may be the very important one of supporting your child's confidence and building up all his other skills. If your child is struggling with emotional problems, and you have tried everything but feel that you are making no progress at all, you may want to seek an independent counsellor. (See the Resources for information on the kind of professionals who could help.)

Making the decision that someone else will be better equipped to help your child in a particular situation is not an admission of failure – sometimes it will be the very best route to take.

For your information

The Department of Education and Science issued a booklet in 1992 on *Children with special needs – a guide for parents*. If you suspect that your child may be dyslexic, then you could get practical advice from:

British Dyslexia Association, 98 London Road, Reading RG1 5AU. Tel: 0734 668271/2.

Helping your child to study

Everything we have said about learning applies, of course, to the study of particular subjects as well as to coping with new skills like reading. You can help your child by encouraging her, by creating a peaceful atmosphere for her to study in and by helping with the inevitable practice.

Using knowledge and skills

Practice and practical use are central to learning. The striking point about highly talented children and young people is that they have been willing to spend many hours practising their skills. This is equally true of chess prodigies, tennis players and musicians. Talent is necessary but this will not develop without masses of practice.

You can help your children by encouraging them to repeat and to use facts and ideas until these have taken a firm hold in their memory. This is often best done by talking out loud – for example, repeating the times tables until they flow correctly. Learning ideas can be helped by asking children to repeat the idea back to you, or to explain a complicated skill, such as how to tell the time using their own words. Be ready to chat with your children about what they have learned whenever they feel like it. Conversation is a good way of helping children to make links between different bits of information and the ideas they are forming. The whole point is to encourage your children to be active learners rather than sit-back passive learners, because active learning is much more effective.

Activity to help your child learn to spell

A good system to aid learning is the simple: Look, Cover and try, Test.

1 Look   Get children to write out the words they are learning – these may come home in the form of spelling homework. Encourage them to take a good look at the words.

2 Cover and try   Children should look at one word at a time, cover the word with a scrap of paper, write out the word as they believe it is spelled and then check this themselves against the original. Children should then run through this a few times until they feel pretty sure they know how to spell these words.

3 Test   Take away their spelling list and test them by reading out the words one at a time. They should write each word down as you go. If they want to spell out loud, without writing, let them. But this is harder to do, so don't let them get disheartened if they need to write the word, for this is the more usual way. It is also a good idea for you to start the habit of reading out the words in a different order to the original list.

4 Run through again   Children should then practise again any words that are causing them trouble and you should test them again – using the same sequence.

5 Reinforce   Leave a gap of a day – or at least a few hours – and test them again.

The same kind of approach will work for memorising other information like dates, capital cities and so on.

Books for you

You will be more able to help your child if you unravel any of your own confusions first. It may help you to get a book or two that will guide you through spelling or maths.

For example, *The Usborne Book of Better English* by Robyn Gee and Carol Watson (Usborne, 1983) is an easy read on the maze of English spelling, punctuation and grammar. It combines information with digestible explanations and gives some short exercises, too. You could find most of the things you wanted to know about how English works and were too embarrassed to ask.

Some parents feel uncertain of their ground with mathematics, if for no other reason than teaching methods have changed since their own school days. *Help your child with maths* by Alan Graham (Fontana, 1983) is written in simple language, and unless you are already a confident mathematician, it will almost certainly help you to understand some of the ideas that passed you by in your school years and will take you and your child into the teenage years.

Working at home

At this age your children may not have any homework from school. However, some primary schools – state and private – do start children with small amounts of work to do at home. This may include:

- gathering information for a project;
- writing down a few ideas;
- finishing off a piece of work; or
- learning spellings or times tables.

Getting your child to complete any homework may be an uphill struggle but this is not necessarily so. Parents and teachers sometimes forget that children can enjoy studying. They can be thrilled at learning something new and by getting better at a subject or skill that they have already learned. The full spectrum of this covers much more than conventionally academic subjects.

Using workbooks

Whether or not your children have homework, you may decide to help them by using workbooks with them. There is a wide range of booklets for number work, writing, reading and other aspects of primary school study. Any good bookshop will have a range and the large toy stores often have a stand. Even smaller shops may have a small selection amongst the stationery, magazines or toys.

There are a great many series on sale now and it is best that you make your own selection. However, from our own experience we would suggest you have a good look inside the booklets before you buy. Make sure the content and level of difficulty suits your child. Some workbooks have a suggested age range for different parts of a series. Look at the contents, too, as some have unnecessarily complicated exercises under the guise of fun. If you can't follow what is wanted, you won't be able to help your child.

Some recent series have the words 'National Curriculum' as part of the title. By all means buy these if they suit, but remember that the National Curriculum represents what is regarded as the best educational practice of recent years. The content and methods are not all brand new, so you can safely use other workbook series, especially those published within the second half of the 1980s.

Once you are buying for seven-year-olds and older, make sure the booklet gives you the answers to any exercises, otherwise you will spend precious time working these out. Some have a pull-out answer sheet, which is handy because you remove this and your child cannot take a crafty look. We were caught out by one series that sold the answers in a completely separate booklet – doubling the real cost. You can save money by re-using booklets. Get your older child to fill in the answers in pencil, so that you can erase them and re-use the booklet with a younger child.

An encouraging environment for study

From now, through to the teenage years, you can help your child by trying to make it easier for them to study at home. Your five to elevens should not be studying for long hours after school, but any work they are doing – reading, memorising, music practice – should be mixed with relaxation, exercise, and fresh air.

Children will flourish if given challenge and stimulation for their developing brain power. If they are pushed to ridiculous lengths to study they will rebel, now or later. The checklist below could help you look at your home as a help or a hindrance to study for your child.

Checklist: Making home-study easier

Your children will need:

- A clear area to work on and to spread out over, such as a table top or desk.
- A separate room if possible. This could be their bedroom, or another room not being used by the rest of the family. However, this is not always possible.
- A good light so that they can see easily, even when they are leaning over their work.
- A store of paper, pencils, eraser etc. and basic reference books, like a children's dictionary.
- Peace and quiet, although some children work better with music or the radio in the background. Some claim that they want the television on but it does distract them. You will see through experimenting and by the quality of their work whether absolute quiet or some noise is better for your child for studying.
- A parent close to hand – for support, questions and help with memorising, if required.

Learning how to plan work

Primary schools nowadays emphasise project work and this draws on the skills of organisation and planning. Children do not necessarily see the need to plan, so you might have to point this out, just as you may also need, later, to warn your teenagers that they have to revise for exams. Even adults can realise to their frustration that if only they had thought about a complete project first, then they would not have spent so long on what turned out to be only a small part of it.

Projects and topics

Chat with your children about their initial ideas for a project. Talk about the main aims of the project, what they want to say, and where the information will come from.

Part of the planning process is working out which resources will be helpful. The skill, of course, is to draw from other resources but not to copy them wholesale. Your children may bring some books home from school, but it will be useful if you can help them to browse through other books as well. Introduce them to your local library and explain how to find different kinds of books.

You may have a range of books that you own. Encyclopedias and other reference books from your childhood can be useful. Don't automatically throw them out as inevitably old fashioned, but if you are using reference books which are over twenty to thirty years old, you will need to watch out for: advances in science, although basics are the same; changes in names of countries; and different perspectives on some periods of history.

Writing

Introduce your children to the idea of a plan for ordering what they want to write. Does one idea or piece of information need to come before another one? Would illustrations help their topic? Show them how to prepare rough notes for ideas and information, and encourage them to draft their work in this way. In a medium- to long-term project, the allocation of time will be important. How long can they allow for gathering ideas and information? How long for actually writing the material? How long for producing the final version?

Speaking

Schools often encourage children to talk to a group or to present work in school assemblies. Planning something to be spoken works in much the same way as written material. You can discuss the following with your children:

- What the topic of their talk is.
- How much time they have to speak.
- What is likely to interest the people they will speak to.
- What are the five main things they want to say?
- Do they want to hold up anything to show to the group? If so, make sure that it is big enough for everyone to see easily.

Children do not need to rehearse a speech word for word, although some feel more confident if they do. They need a clear plan of the points they will make and probably a firm decision on their first sentence, which will engage the audience's attention, and their last sentence – the final message they leave their audience. Children may need to practise making their voices carry, taking breaths at sensible moments in what they are saying, and speaking at a steady pace. Talks to an audience are best delivered at a pace that is slower than many people speak in everyday conversation.

For your information

As your children get older you may welcome ideas for more challenging study. Try *Study skills for GCSE and A level* by Michael Montgomery (Letts Educational, 1991).

Tests and exams

The whole business of testing generates a lot of anxiety and argument. However, a combination of continuous assessment and tests in school can give valuable information to children themselves and to parents on how their children are doing. A great deal depends on giving accurate and constructive feedback to children and their parents. (Remember what we said earlier about what makes encouraging feedback.) Teachers and parents need to know how children are progressing in key skills like reading, writing, number work, conversational skills and other topics. Any test should inform the child, teacher and parent of how the child is managing right now. It's a snapshot in time.

Children who emerge strongly from any kind of assessment deserve praise for their hard work so far and encouragement to keep them tackling the new work ahead. Children who are weak in a skill or a subject area will probably already realise this. Putting your finger on this through assessment does not dishearten children, unless it is delivered with a 'you're hopeless' message and there is no effort to help a child with specific suggestions on how to improve.

Helping children with tests

First of all, find out all you can about assessment within the National Curriculum. The Department of Education and Science issued a leaflet in 1992, *How is your child doing at school – a parent's guide to tests and reports for 7-year-olds*. At the time of writing, in 1992, there were still changes in the programme of assessment, so you need to be willing to update yourself. You can read information about the National Curriculum as a whole. For example: the Department for Education booklet, *Your child and the National Curriculum*, 1992; and the Letts' *Parents' Guides to the National Curriculum – Primary School and Secondary School*. These are, of course, in addition to any information or displays that your own children's school makes available.

If you would like to help your child at home, there are some good booklets around. Remember the practical suggestions we made earlier about using workbooks. As with anything else you do with your children, don't overdo it. Be very encouraging so that your child emerges from sessions at the kitchen table feeling that he has made progress. If your children have been working in a poorly controlled open classroom, then the best help you can give them is practice in sitting still and seeing a task through to the end. Look back at what we said earlier about how long children are likely to be able to concentrate at different ages.

Introduce your children to sensible test techniques, and share these basic tips:

- Listen carefully to any spoken instructions. Read the questions carefully. There are no marks for an answer that would have been correct for a different question.
- Don't spend too long on any one question. If you are getting nowhere, move on and then come back to your unanswered questions later, if you have time.
- Don't give up if there is a run of hard questions, because there may be some later on that you can answer.
- It is worth guessing, if you have a feeling about the right answer. At the moment, your children are unlikely to be taking tests where wrong answers are penalised with actually losing a mark. If in doubt, check this point.

If your child is dyslexic, he or she will have difficulty where written instructions and answers are part of a test. Keep pushing the school for special help in study skills and support for tests and exams.

For your information

We would recommend the book *Back to Basics – your child's progress from 7 to 13* by Michael Nathenson (Fontana, 1985). If you wish, this book will enable you to give your children tests in Mathematics and English. The author explains carefully how to do this properly. This is the only book we have found so far that allows you to make sense of your child's score against averages for their age.

Worries and pressures

Your children will probably worry about schoolwork and tests to some extent. Indeed, if they are too relaxed about tests, they may not summon up that edge to give of their best. You can help them get used to taking tests by giving them practice at home. Show them how to put the test techniques to work, and also:

- Work hard to keep your anxiety under wraps. Although you will be concerned on their behalf, try to avoid making this your child's worry as well. This is as true of your general concerns about their schoolwork as for exams. If you can do something about your concern, then get on with doing this.
- Help your child to take a break. Make sure that schoolwork or practice for dance or karate exams is not getting on top of them. Suggest they get some fresh air, go to the cinema, or do something just for fun.
- Encourage your children to develop an interest and liking for subjects for their own sake and not just as something to study to pass a test. It is a broader interest that will keep them motivated as they face the greater demands of the teenage years in terms of exams.
- Don't offer large incentives, cash or presents, to your child for achieving high marks or passing a test. Although parents hope this will encourage hard work, it usually only adds to the pressure on the child. Even worse is cutting their pocket money for not passing a test.
- Don't compare your children unfavourably with their brothers, sisters, friends or relatives. If they need to be firmly encouraged to pull their socks up, then work at this on an individual basis. If you ask them why they can't be hard workers like Kimberley or Rafat, this will only encourage a backlash on the so-called good children. Likewise, a line such as 'I don't understand why you're no good at music. All the males in our family are good at music' is a disaster.

Final thoughts

The best way you can help your child is by giving her your time and your encouragement. You will be a support if you are willing to think things over and can learn to look through your child's eyes. From maths to family relationships, from issues of birth and death to why you should iron some sweatshirts inside out, the difficulty is often to spot what your child does not understand. You have to use your adult experience to work out 'What does my child have to grasp before they can . . .'

Going back to the basics helps to reduce your own frustrations, for example when you have explained something five times in words of one syllable and the face in front of you is still as blank as ever. It is terribly easy for you to miss a step you know so well, and take it for granted that your child will know it too. You need a calm moment to stand back quietly to identify what your child is missing.

A tremendously positive change over the last ten to fifteen years has been a more general recognition by professionals of all kinds that parents are central to their children's lives. You are often the best person to help your child. You are the only person who has a hope of coordinating all the different parts of your child's life.

CHAPTER THREE

Change and your family

The only unchanging fact of life is that things will change. People often think of change as unpleasant and out of their control. It can be, but many changes are less dramatic and you will make some changes happen yourself. You may decide to scrap an old washing machine for a better one. You may move your children's dinner time from five o'clock to seven o'clock as they get older. Making changes does not, of course, always go smoothly. You may have very good intentions about listening more to your children, but find it difficult in practice. Your children may agree in theory that it's mean of them to expect you to clean up the bathroom after them, but getting them to stop behaving like slobs takes time and hard work.

Some changes are inevitable, whether you like it or not. Your children will grow older and will want to do some things without you. They will make friends whose opinions carry more weight than yours. One day they will leave home. You cannot stop these things happening; but you can do your best to adjust to them. Some changes may be forced upon you. You know they may happen but you hope they will not happen to you, or not yet. Many families have to cope with one or two breadwinners being made redundant. Families are split by divorce and have to adjust to new partners and perhaps new children. You may grieve for the death of your own parents at a time when you are still finding out what parent-hood means to you.

Making and accepting changes can be difficult. Sometimes it is painful. However, you may be more able to deal with the changes forced upon you, if you are willing to work for changes in your family life that you want to make happen.

Planning change

There may be some aspects of your family life with which you are not entirely happy, and, you may choose to make some changes. Perhaps there are some things that you are uncomfortable with, but have learned to live with. Either way, you are unlikely to bring about change overnight. How you approach the business of attempting to make any change in family life is very important. The section below offers some guidelines.

Steps in making changes

You won't be able to tackle too many changes all at once. In one of your rare peaceful moments, think over the following:

1 What do you want to change?   To begin, make your own list. The different items will probably vary on how vague an idea they are and what is a realistic time-scale. For example:

- I want the children to stop arguing.
- I need some time to myself.
- I want the rest of the family to help out with keeping the house tidy.
- I want us to spend more time together as a family.
- I want a clear agreement over pocket money. The children nag us for more money when they have spent this week's amount.
- I want to spend more time chatting with the children.

2 Choose one thing for your attention first   Let's say you feel that life would be a lot more tolerable if you could guarantee a bit of time to yourself for doing something you would like to do.

3 Think about the present situation and how you would like things to be   Get clear in your mind what is the matter with the situation at the moment. Think positively and realistically about how you would like it to be different, and recognise that this is only an opinion – other family members may disagree. In this case, you might want hours to yourself, but you know that this is not really practicable. Therefore . . .

4 Define your goal to be realistic and achievable   Perhaps you feel that a guaranteed fifteen minutes a day to do exactly what you want, without any interruptions, would be a real help. You would also like a longer stretch – an hour or so – once a week. This does not seem unduly greedy to you. Perhaps the last straw is that nobody even lets you get your coat off when you come in from work before they all appear to be at you.

5 Talk this over with the rest of the family   Take a calm moment and explain what is getting you down and that you want to find a way through. You appreciate that the rest of the family wants your time and attention but you feel that you never get any peace.

6 Be flexible about how you achieve your goal   Make it easy for the others to help. When would be the best time for you to have your fifteen minutes of peace and your longer stretch? If you have a partner, does he or she feel cheated out of peaceful time as well? Do the children complain that you interrupt them when they are busy?

7 Reaching a family deal   Between children and adults, you can reach a firm agreement about what could work for your family. This is more likely to work if everyone involved gives a bit and gets in return – a family deal. For example, it is understood that you can have fifteen minutes unbothered when you come in from work, but you promise that you will not stretch this out. The children can put the kitchen timer on to make sure that you don't. If you have a partner, you arrange to return the compliment for him or her.

8 Hold to the deal The best family deal in the world will not magically remove all the trouble. Give it time and encourage everyone to stick to their part of the bargain and stick to yours. Say thanks for leaving you in peace.

9 What next? After some success, look at your list again and try another item. Since quite a lot of everyday family difficulties are about communication and negotiation, you may find that the lessons learned over one issue may give you a headstart on another.

Progressively move, one at a time, to more difficult issues. Success breeds success. Most changes that you make will work, *provided* you have the support of others, keep at it and ensure that you encourage all actions by your family that support the change. Part of this has to be talking things through in your family.

For your information

There are two books which could be helpful if you are willing to look at your own behaviour as well as how your children act. Please don't be put off by the titles; the contents of the books are practical and sensible: *Happy children – a challenge to parents* by Rudolf Dreikurs (published by Fontana, this comes in and out of print); and *Parent effectiveness training in action* by Thomas Gordon (Bantam, 1976).

Family discussions

Disagreements without fighting

Parents set the pattern for how disagreements, even mild differences of opinion, are settled in any family. If you won't listen or lose your temper at the drop of a hat, so will your children. They will have learned to behave that way from you. Children often have less patience, so it is even more important that they see you able to handle disagreements. You are then on stronger ground if your nine- or ten-year-old starts importing aggressive playground methods into your home.

Some differences of opinion between parents should be sorted out away from the children. You then present a united front, having made whatever compromises were necessary behind closed doors. If children see both parents arguing over house rules, they may exploit this for their own benefit. The other possibility is that they may be distressed by the argument and leap to the conclusion that divorce is imminent. However your family is made up, by eight to nine years of age, your children will almost certainly have a few friends whose parents are divorced. Let your children see you make up and apologise if a disagreement has got out of hand in front of them.

Family meetings

From time to time it helps to have a family meeting. It does not have to be dauntingly formal; you don't put up notices or take minutes. You do need to sit down and listen to one another. You might have a family discussion for any of the following:

- To swap ideas for what you will eat for dinner over the next week. The cook in the family may be fed up with people moaning when he or she has no hope of changing the evening meal.
- To find out which friend your child would like to stay late with next Friday because both Daddy and Mummy have meetings.
- To ask what your child would like to do over the school holidays.
- To tell the children what is happening next weekend.
- To discuss why your children only seem to remember they have homework late in the evening and what can be done about it.

You would not have a family meeting for ticking off one of your children or for discussing one child's problem with the playground bully – this is something you would discuss with the child concerned. Basically, don't have a whole family discussion, unless the issue is clearly a family one.

A family meeting is a kind of business meeting – family business – and there are sensible ways to run any meeting. The guide for family meetings below provides some tips.

A guide to running useful family meetings

- Don't have too many meetings. Have one because there is a good reason and because you need all the family together for the discussion.
- A family meeting deserves everyone's full attention, so switch off the television and don't do other things like read the newspaper at the same time. The same rules apply for adults and children.
- Don't have an enormous agenda. Aim to cover no more than one or two issues. Discuss those fully and finish before your children's attention span is exhausted. If necessary, finish another day.
- Be clear about what kind of meeting it is. In families as in business, there are different kinds of meetings. Be straight about this. The options may be:
  - This is completely open as a decision, what you want is what we will do.
  - We want your ideas and depending on expense, time etc. we will pick from amongst your suggestions.
  - We want your ideas but we adults will make the final decision.
  - We need to solve this problem. These are the possibilities we can see. Which would you prefer or can you see any other way to resolve the problem?

- This is a decision we have made as your parents. We want to explain our reasons, but there is no changing the actual decision.

What infuriates adults and children alike is to be given the impression that what they say could influence a decision, only later to discover that the decision had already been made and the meeting was for 'information only'.

- Make sure that everyone in the family gets a chance to say their bit. The more vocal ones should not ride rough-shod over the quieter ones. Check out, by asking each person directly, what they think and whether they agree and have understood.

- When you have finished, have an adult or child summarise the decisions or information and make sure everyone has understood the main points. This is to avoid future moans of 'Nobody told me' or 'But I thought that we agreed . . .'

- When you are finished, close the meeting and let everyone go about their own individual business.

Initially, it is most likely that the adults will ask for five minutes of full attention for a family meeting. However, your children will begin to ask for their slot when they see that it is a good way of airing their concerns. Meetings can take place at any convenient time – even over a family meal, so long as this doesn't mean that slow eaters don't complete their meal.

Family rules and change

Children aged between five and eleven are better able to do more, without your direct involvement, than when they were younger. However, they still need a sense of an ordered life. They need to know what is acceptable and what is not. It makes sense to develop some boundaries and limits; rules within which they can work.

As you set and negotiate the rules, you teach your children what you believe to be important. You can be clear about your own values, which may come from general convictions about what is right or from specific religious beliefs. Eventually your children will decide whether they agree with you or not.

All families have rules, both shared and unspoken. Even those families who say they don't have rules, do. The rule is that there are no rules, or at least no agreed rules. In defining limits within your family it is sensible to err on the side of too few rules rather than too many. The more rules there are, the more likely it is that none will be seen as important or that family members will feel weighed down by them. Any house rules should be clearly stated and possible to follow without requiring ludicrously high standards of good behaviour. The rules must be applied consistently and, of course, adults must obey their own house rules.

Realistic house rules

Why not think through the assumptions that you have about the way you want your children to behave? Include both the spoken and the unspoken rules. It may be helpful to think in terms of major family activities, for example:

- Mealtimes at home and eating out.
- Eating sweets and snacks.
- Bedtime and adults' right to some evening time.
- Tidiness, and any different requirements for different rooms. For example do you have, or want to have, an adult room from which all child paraphernalia is banned permanently?
- Rooms or tables where activities like pasting or cutting can take place and places where they are forbidden.
- Privacy, both yours and your children's.
- Considerate treatment of each other.

You might like to pool your family's perceptions of what these rules are, and discuss them. Are there too many or too few? Which are helpful, and which are not? Are adults obeying the relevant rules as well? Are there some rules which are hard to keep, and how can this be made easier? Do you expect visiting children or adults to obey the house rules? How do you handle rule-breaking?

All families need clear and agreed rules. If you have trial rules, then when are these to be confirmed or abandoned? It's wise to review any house rules from time to time. This is particularly true if rules are not working or are seen as too much trouble for their importance. Your children are getting older and so some rules may be inappropriate. Families may need a fresh agreement precisely because the children are older.

Children's responsibilities

With smaller families becoming more usual, many parents have slipped into a habit of doing almost all the domestic chores. If you have more than two or three children, it is almost certain that you will expect them to help out – life would be impossible otherwise. Encouraging, or even insisting, that children pitch in on some of the household tasks that involve them is a wise move, otherwise you may produce lazy children who haven't a clue how to take care of themselves and little understanding of how much effort is involved.

You may be disappointed if you expect children to accept new home responsibilities without an argument. Children, like adults, are going to be very happy to have someone else pick up their clothes, clear their plate and check on their games kit. It's a good deal – why change it? However, you will sometimes be pleasantly surprised when your children cooperate happily. There are many jobs that children can do safely. They don't need to learn a new skill, but just to remember to do it. You don't have to be of mature years to be capable of tidying up or putting dirty washing in the basket. Other tasks, like washing the car, cooking or ironing are new skills. You will need to teach your children how to do them.

Children come to household jobs fresh. They often enjoy learning how to do new and grown-up things and being able to say 'Daddy and I made . . .' or 'Mummy let me do it myself . . .' Children like to show that they are becoming competent in more and more things. You may seriously underestimate that a major attraction for children is spending time with you doing a task, rather than cooling their heels until you've finished it alone. You have to guard against getting in the way of your child's enthusiasm for tasks you now find boring. Children can be a real help as well as good company, and they may even enjoy doing tasks you dislike. So, if your children are avoiding helping out, it is worth checking whether you are making it hard for them to get involved with you when they actually want to help.

Encouraging children to help

You're not running a Victorian workhouse just because you want your children to develop into working members of your household. If you involved your under-fives in some of your everyday activities around the house, you may be well on the way by now. Let your children help as much as possible when they want to. This can be a relatively painless route into developing them as responsible members of the household.

Make it clear what you do expect them to do. This does not mean rotas or pages of tasks and related punishments, but it does mean telling your children simply and patiently how you want them to help out. Do your level best to repeat your requests – as you will have to many times – as calmly and as close to normal volume as you can manage. Make sure that your requests are realistic. Life will be awful for you and your children if you demand very high standards or never allow any leeway. For example, it is very unlikely that your children will manage to keep their rooms tidy all the time. Do be prepared to reach a compromise and stick to your side of the bargain. If the deal is that their room is tidy every

Saturday morning, then bite your lip over the piles of mess on Wednesday. You may have to clear a passage through to make the bed, but if you nag them about the disgusting state of their room, you are breaking the deal.

Make the effort to notice when children do carry out their tasks or help you without being asked. It is very discouraging for children, as it is for adults, to feel that people only take the trouble to say something if they're shirking. Just because somebody should do something doesn't mean you don't thank them. Your 'well done' will tell your son that you have noticed that you don't have to remind him anymore to hang up his coat. Your daughter will appreciate a 'thank you' when she clears away her plate and per-haps other people's as well.

You would be wise to avoid complicated systems of payment. You may have an agreement to give extra pocket money for a few clearly defined jobs, but don't fall into the trap of paying your child (with money, gifts or extra privileges) for every job he helps out with. Pay-ment or treats are best used for jobs that are either time-consuming and ones that your child does not like doing, or special jobs that you would not normally expect him or her to do within your family's rules. It's fair that you should be able to ask your son or daughter to lay the table some days or run a message to someone in another room, without the demand of 'What's in it for me if I do?'

Decide what happens if children don't carry out their household responsibilities. The negative consequences do not have to be dire, but they do have to be consistently applied. For example, if you have a rule that children clear their dishes after a meal, escapees should have to come back to do it NOW, regardless of whether they have rushed off to watch their favourite programme. Or, perhaps it should be understood that rooms not tidied by a child are tidied by a parent who may make unwelcome decisions about what gets thrown away. Some consequences follow naturally from what your child has or has not done. For example, toys left all over the floor are sometimes trodden on – not deliberately – but as a direct conse-quence of them being on the floor where people walk.

Change and crisis

Family life can become very hard when change is forced upon you, or a change that you predicted turns out to be more far-reaching and distressing than you ever expected. It may be redundancy, the death of a close relative, separation and divorce, or a major illness for you or your child. As hard as it can be for you, you must not leave your children out of what is happening. Even if they do not fully understand what is going on, children are sensitive to family atmosphere. You will not fool them that everything is normal if it is not.

Take time and explain to your children what has happened or is still happening. Be honest with them about your feelings, without loading those feelings onto them. If you have lost someone dear to you, don't try to pretend that you are not distressed – this won't be credible, because your behaviour will change. It will also give children the misleading message that adults are never upset. You may try not to break down in front of your children, as this might disturb them. However, be prepared to say a little about how you are feeling. Your children will know you are upset, and quite often can be surprisingly sensitive to your needs.

Telling your children

Probably the worst thing you can do is to avoid talking with your children when some disturbing change has hit your family or is about to arrive.

When should we tell the children? As soon as possible. Your children have a right to know what is happening; they will sense from the family atmosphere that something is amiss.

What should we tell them? Practical, simple details are best. They need to know how their lives will be affected by this event. You need to manage their expectations of what *will* happen, what *might*, and what *will not*. If one of the family has to go into hospital, your children may be unrealistically worried and you may be able to reassure them. If the crisis is the death of a loved grandparent, this experience may bring home to your children that people we love are not with us forever and this is hard. You will need to answer their questions as they occur.

Who should tell them? Preferably the member of the family best able to explain and talk calmly. This need not necessarily be the one most affected. If a parent has been made redundant, he or she may be too worried or angry to talk clearly.

How do we tell them? In a private moment, when you are not rushed, using simple words. Tell them slowly and carefully what is happening and then give them space to reply and ask questions if they wish. Make it clear to your children that you will listen to them if they would prefer to talk later.

Using books to help

There are many good books, including fiction, about the normal ups and downs of everyday life. You may have used picture books with your children when they were younger, to prepare them for the arrival of a new baby or everyday events like going to the dentist.

Some older children are helped through painful emotions by reading about a fictional character who has lost a loved grandparent or whose parents are divorcing. You will need to decide from your knowledge of your child whether this is likely to be a help. However, giving your child a book to read must be something you do *as well as* talking with your child and cuddling, not instead of.

Family break-up

An increasing number of families will be disrupted by separation or divorce. This will be upsetting for adults and children – even if the break up is not actually hostile. You can divorce from a partner and stop being married. You cannot stop being a parent.

Sometimes children are relieved that parents are breaking up, because home has become a thoroughly miserable place. However, often children will not want their parents to separate, hoping that the adults can somehow fix it, as they fix so many things in life.

Children's needs when parents separate

Professionals who work as conciliators in marriage breakdowns confirm that children need reassurance on some specific issues. These are:

- Clear information and explanations from their parents about what is happening now and what will happen in the future.
- An obvious effort from parents to recognise and understand the children's own feelings, and their right to have them.
- Reassurance of their parents' love for the children whatever has happened between the adults.
- Relief from the conflict between the parents. A family history of rows or cold silences takes its toll on children.
- Freedom to continue a relationship with both parents which involves seeing them both – without being asked to take sides, being bribed, or cross-questioned about the other.
- Relief from any guilt feelings that somehow they, as children, have contributed to the break-up.

For your information

Family life is not all wine and roses, even when parents stay together happily. You might enjoy the book *Families and how to survive them* by Robin Skynner and John Cleese (Methuen, 1983) and be provoked into some new thoughts about how your own family works.

Stepfamilies experience all the ups and downs of family life with the additional adjustments of being related together in different ways. Try two books written by Erica De'Ath:

Step-parenting (Family Doctor Publication, 1988) and *A baby of our own, a new baby in a stepfamily* (1992). Both of these are available from the National Stepfamily Association, 72 Willesden Lane, London NW6 7TA.

Family life/school life

Your relationship with your children's school is a major part of your life now. Part of this involves choosing a school (where you have a realistic choice of more than one) and another part is working hard to make the moves from home to school, nursery school to primary school and on to the secondary stage as smooth as you can.

Helping your child with the change

It is generally easier for children who have attended the nursery class of their primary school to make a painless move to the reception class. However, some children become convinced that the next stage is dreadfully different, even when all sections of a primary school are in the same building.

Most schools work hard to make the transition as smooth as possible, both for parents and their children, and you can help by accepting any invitation to visit with your child, before the first day. The visit should help your child, and may also allay some of your own fears. The guide below makes some suggestions for easing your child into school.

And so to school . . .

You can prepare your children to some extent by:

- Chatting to them about what to expect and putting to rest any unrealistic worries.

- Working with them on any practical skills that they still find difficult or worrisome. For five-year-olds, this might be their ability to dress and undress, to manage going to the toilet without help, and to eat dinner with ease. (Some schools make a bigger issue than others about use of a knife and fork, which after all is not a universal method of eating food.)
- Reassuring them that their first teachers will not expect them to be able to do everything straightaway.
- Perhaps buying children something, like a new school bag, to mark this important change in their life.

Both on the night before and on the first day itself, look confident, smile, act like it is going to be fine. Say cheerfully that you are looking forward to hearing all about it at coming home time. Inspire their confidence.

Getting involved in school life

In choosing how far you get involved with the school, part of your decision is what and how much you want to do. You also need to consider what your children want you to do and how they would rather you behaved. For example, your son may want you to come on the school trip; your daughter may be happier if you keep away. They may be proud of you when you run the school drama club; they may cringe with embarrassment when you shout from the sidelines on sports day. If you talk with your children you will have a chance of finding out. You will need consciously to balance your own inclinations with your child's preferences.

Contact with teachers

Do take any opportunities to chat with teachers as one adult to another. It will help you, your child and your child's teacher if you can have a friendly working relationship. You may meet teachers more formally through school open evenings, which provide an opportunity to get an overall picture of your child. Do take the chance to see your child's work and to look at general displays that illustrate teaching methods and the themes that your child's class is following that term. This will help you to support your child at home and may unravel some of the mystery when your child seems to be confused. However, you may want to talk with your child's class teacher about something specific. This will probably be about a problem that's bothering you or your child. You will want to discuss this in more privacy than the playground or open corridor offers. The guide below gives some practical tips on making the best of any kind of meeting.

The three 'P's of school parenting

You will have the best chance of emerging satisfied with any meeting if you allow for the three 'P's – preparation, politeness, and persistence.

Preparation
- Prepare for an open evening or a meeting that you have requested by thinking about the questions to which you require answers.
- If you know you tend to get tongue-tied or distracted by side issues in these meetings, then it's a good idea to write yourself a short list of key questions or reminders.
- Talk over the forthcoming meeting with your child. What questions would he suggest? Does he have any concerns? What pieces of his work does he particularly want you to look at? Your child's main concern, of course, can be that you will not say something embarrassing.

Politeness
- Even if you are feeling frustrated with the class teacher, it is courteous to try to work something out with him or her first and not to go straight to the headteacher or head of department.

- Approach the meeting as an opportunity to explain your concern. Be clear about what concerns you – your son is claiming he is 'no good' at maths, your daughter seems to be spending a lot of her school time helping out less able children . . . Don't lay blame, even if you do have a firm opinion on this. Focus on what is happening, rather than speculating about why.
- Do allow for the possibility that teachers may actually be nervous of you. You are probably more daunting than your children. Even the headteacher may be wary if you have asked for an appointment to talk. She or he may be expecting a blast.

Persistence

- Be ready to repeat your concern in different words if the teacher seems to be failing to understand or dodging the issue.
- Stress that you want to work something out *with* your child's teacher, while emphasising that you are not happy for things to continue as they are.
- You do not have to be satisfied with banal 'It'll all be all right in the end' messages.
- If you are getting nowhere, or the nub of the difficulty seems to be school policy, or lack of it, the time may have come to talk with the headteacher or a parent governor.

Finally

Do take the time and trouble to have a conversation with the class teacher or the headteacher when you are pleased about something. Teachers are people with feelings too, and they deserve some encouragement as they are often on the receiving end of a lot of criticism – rather like parents, in fact. Also, on purely selfish grounds, you will have more chance of getting somewhere when you have a concern if you have established yourself as a parent who does more than just complain.

School is a major part of life for you and your child. This need not exclude you, although you have to adjust to your new position. As you enter your child's school it is very possible that memories of your own school days will come flooding back. It can be most disconcerting to have feelings from the child that you once were, becoming entangled with your adult self. It may take time and a bit of thought to move into an adult role in relation to school on behalf of your child.

For your information

Even if you are only choosing between a couple of schools, the book *Choosing a state school* by Caroline Cox, Robert Balchin and John Marks (Century Hutchinson, 1989) could help you prepare yourself for what you want to know and look out for. Also *Help your child through school* by Jennie and Lance Lindon (Headway, 1994) is a helpful and practical book on working in cooperation with your child's school.

Final thoughts

Change in your family is inevitable. You have already faced and handled making changes as your children have grown from babies into toddlers and into young children. In the early years of childhood you had no choice but to keep adjusting as your child developed new abilities and interests, some of which were potentially dangerous without your swift intervention.

Change is not always threatening; it can be both positive and negative. Planned changes can improve family life as you support each other. Facing and dealing with unplanned events successfully can strengthen a family. The Chinese character for change is the combination of their glyphs for opportunity and hidden danger or pain. In managing change, both of these factors are equally true. The task of parents is to help reduce the danger and pain – to keep it short, or less sharp – and to build on the opportunities for learning and growing. Teaching your children to cope constructively with change will be a valuable gift to them for their teenage and adult years.

For your information

Sometimes adults find it hard to cope because too much is happening all at once. Even the most capable people have a limit to what they can manage. You might find it helpful to read about sources of stress and what you could do for yourself. Try either or both of the following books: *Living with stress* by Cary Cooper, Rachel Cooper and Lynn Eaker (Penguin Health, 1988) and *Stressmanship* by Audrey Livingston Booth (Severn House, 1985).

CHAPTER FOUR

Communication within the family

Basic communication

Being able to communicate and to understand what other people are saying or want is central to family life and to your child's development. There is much more to this than just what is said out loud.

Body language

Your child has been transmitting and receiving on the body language wavelength since babyhood. This does not stop with the first spoken words. Body language – movement of body, limbs, eyes, facial expression and tone of voice – remains extremely powerful throughout life. If the two do not match, both adults and children tend to trust what they see rather than what is said. You may underestimate your children's awareness of the unspoken messages. Adults are often unaware of how much they depend on the non-verbal side of communication. Words add to body language to build the total message. Children are no different from adults, with the exception that they may need to depend more on the unspoken messages when they literally do not understand your words.

In times of family upheaval, parents sometimes assume that, if nothing is said in words, then children will not realise that something is amiss. However, children look and listen. They see your expressions and they guess at what you are feeling. They may not be able to put their worries into words but they know something is not right. They will reach their own conclusions on the basis of what little information they can glean. Unfortunately, they often decide wrongly that they have caused your upset by something they have done. Even in less dramatic circumstances, your children will have good working theories of how your behaviour changes when you are worried or under pressure. Ask them, they have expertise from watching you. For example, our son's view of Jennie when she is working too hard is that 'she makes up more rules and stops doing the silly stuff' – this being the larking about and teasing that is usual in less stressful times. He's right too.

Spoken language

By five years of age, your children have already made great strides in spoken language. They may use more than one language with confidence. However, as articulate as they may be, they will not always understand. They still have a lot to learn in terms of ideas as well as the actual words.

Spoken language has two aspects. First, there is the ability to talk and to make yourself understood. Second is the ability to listen to others and to understand them. Your child needs both – to transmit and to receive.

Misunderstandings

However careful you are, communication with children is littered with misunderstandings. At some time all parents will be ready to pull their hair out over the apparent impossibility of getting a simple message through to their children. 'In one ear out the other!' you shout in frustration. Your children in turn will snap at you 'Mum, I've told you a million times . . .' Sometimes, of course, your children weren't listening to you in the first place, and sometimes they genuinely can't follow what you are going on about. But very often you are facing the kind of misunderstanding that also happens regularly between adults. Look at the example below.

Example of misunderstood communication

One Saturday morning . . .

It starts with an idea in your head:	I need Jane's bedroom tidy by the end of the weekend.
What you mean to say is:	Jane, I want you to find a time between now and the end of the weekend to tidy up your room. I appreciate that your room is small and it's hard to find places to put everything away. However, it's a real mess at the moment and I don't have the time to clean it. We went through all this last weekend and I don't want to have a row like then.
The shorter version that you actually said:	Please find time this weekend to tidy your room. I know your room is small, but it's a mess now. I can't clean it. Last weekend we had a row, I don't want us to have another one.

You are speaking face to face with your daughter, but she was thinking of something else when you started talking and she has just had a row with her brother.

What your child actually heard:	. . . this weekend . . . tidy up your room. . . . your room is small but it's a mess now . . . clean it. Last weekend we had a row, I don't want us to have another one.
What she is sure you said:	Your room's filthy! Tidy it up! It's a mess! Clean it! We'll have another row!'

| *So your daughter is now thinking:* | Nag, nag, nag! Rows! What happened to 'please'? I'm supposed to say 'please'! |

We have given a fairly typical example of what can go wrong. It will often happen that your words do not come out quite how you planned. Additionally, whenever there is a bit of past history, your tone of voice may well be sharper than you intend. This is life. You will never get all your communications through perfectly, but you need to do your best, with a realisation that misunderstandings will happen.

Another problem is that children – just like adults – tend to hear what interests them and shut out the boring stuff. So, the mere whisper of 'ice-cream' can be heard from yards away by the same child who ignores an order to 'put on your shoes' yelled from a distance of two feet.

For your information

Adults have serious misunderstandings too. Take a look at *You just don't understand – men and women in conversation* by Deborah Tannen (Virago, 1992).

Conversations and ideas

Good communications in families are fed by regular conversations. The checklist on the next page is designed to help you to assess where your family is at the moment, and to provide some ideas. Fathers may need to pay particular attention here, for, according to a report in *The Times* (June 1991), fathers on average spend just three minutes a day talking with their children.

COMMUNICATION WITHIN THE FAMILY

Do you have a conversational family?

Some things to think about:

Some specific questions about last week
How many times have you had a conversation with your child?
How long, on average, did these last?
What were they about?
What did you learn about your child?
What do you think your child learned about you?
Who tends to start a conversation – you or your child?

Some general questions
Who talks more – you or your child?
If you have more than one child, in what ways are they different? Do they want to talk about different things?
What time of the day do your children tend to want to chat with you? Is it an awkward time, and if so, what can you do about this?
Do you eat meals together and chat over mealtime?
If you have a car, do you tend to play tapes or listen to the radio most of the time? Do you talk together on some journeys?
Do you sometimes switch off the television and talk when you are all together at home?
Do you ask your children for their opinions?
Do your children speak to other members of the family on the phone?

In looking at the checklist, are there any topics of conversation that are rarely discussed? Is it possible to broaden the range of areas covered? Do you wish to make some time to have more conversations?

For your information

If you are a bilingual family, you might be looking for further
practical advice. You could try *Bilingual from birth to teens*
by George Saunders (Avon, 1988). This and other material
is available from Multilingual Matters, Bank House, 8a Hill
Road, Clevedon, Avon BS21 7HH. Tel: 0272 876519.

Learning through conversation

As your children move from five to eleven years of age, some of
the questions they ask will really make you think in order to give
a useful reply. Could you easily answer the following which have
all been asked by children?

- 'How do you grow? Why do you stop growing? Why do plants
  grow, nobody gives them dinner?'
- 'Do you go faster if you run along the corridor when the train
  is moving?'
- 'What makes some clouds black and others white? . . . Why?'
- 'How do deaf people learn sign language? How can they know
  what it means?'
- Or even the apparently simple – 'What exactly do you do in
  your work?'

If you make yourself available to your children for conversation,
you may be cross-questioned on a huge range of ideas. These can
vary from 'What happens when you die?' to 'Why can't I make the
toilet flush when someone else has just flushed it?' On some questions of fact you will know the answer. If you don't, then can you
find out? It is important to be honest about this, for your children
will soon discover if your answer is incorrect. Other questions will
need a statement of your opinion or your belief, for example, 'I
believe in reincarnation but no one alive knows for sure'. It's important that your child distinguishes between these two sorts of frame-
work. There are facts which largely have right answers and there

are beliefs, which are essentially opinions, however strong your faith may be.

Helping children to understand and to learn more can be satisfying and exciting for you. Children question what you take for granted, probing areas that you have never really thought about. This in turn makes you think, which can be fun, although at least some of these insights occur when you are jostling with the chips coming to a dangerous boil or when driving in heavy traffic.

Sometimes you will find that words are expected to carry some very complicated ideas and often they are just not up to it. You need to be ready to show children what you mean as well as just telling them in different ways.

Conversations and problems

If you give attention and affection to your children, they will turn to you in times of trouble. This can be fairly manageable with the under fives – grazed knees, wet trousers, or a snatched toy. However, as they get older, the problems that children bring to you can get more complicated. You may find that some dilemmas are your child's version of areas that you have not resolved fully in your adult life. For example:

- 'He says I've got to ask him to my party or he'll beat me up'; or 'I've got to ask her or she'll be upset.'
- 'I like playing with Amy and Tim but when we play Mums and Dads, they make me be the baby all the time because I'm little.'
- 'They call me names. They know it upsets me and they don't care.'
- 'She keeps borrowing my special crayons. If I say "No", then she tells the teacher I'm selfish.'

It can be more complicated for you to help, because you are not actually there when the problem arises as you often were when they were younger. You are trying to help your child find a way around the problem but he or she is the one who will actually have to do something.

In trying to help their children parents sometimes agonise over what is the right thing to say. There is often no one right answer, although there are more, and less, helpful things to say. Remember that your children will not always expect you to have a solution to their problem. Like adults, they sometimes just feel better for talking about what troubles them.

Helping with problems

First of all, be clear about what will *not* help your child.

Try hard not to feel guilty or distressed yourself   You cannot protect your children against life or make everything all right for them. This is impossible. But you can help them to learn ways of coping and strategies of problem solving that will help them into and during adult life. If you become upset or angry, your children may avoid talking to you again because 'It only upsets them'.

Don't charge in like the cavalry for every problem   There will be times when you and your child will agree that your adult weight has to be brought to bear. Make this a decision to be reached and not an automatic reaction. You want your child to learn confidence, so that he can cope successfully with tricky situations. For him to learn this, you have to let him go it alone sometimes.

There are rarely simple solutions to problems   The problems your child brings to you may sometimes have straightforward answers but you cannot depend on this. If parents insist that every problem has an easy answer or resort to spouting clichés, then they will not help their children. For example, difficulties with other children cannot easily be solved with suggestions of 'Don't play with them then'. Your child will probably come back with 'But they are my friends' or 'There is no one else to play with'. Clichés like 'Sticks and stones may break my bones but words will never hurt me' have been proved wrong by more than one generation of weeping children.

Next, try to work out what *will* help your child.

Listen to what your child is saying   Trained counsellors are taught to listen carefully to what is said, and how it is said. They resist giving swift advice or cross-questioning. They also resist dominating the conversation with personal reminiscences. What happened to you in your childhood can only be of value to your child if she is confident you have tried to understand what is happening to her now.

If your child seems troubled or confused, ask her if there is anything on her mind, encourage her to tell you about it, and listen to what she says. Help her to express what is worrying her by listening more than talking to start with.

See things through your child's eyes   You can do this by reflecting back – summarising what your child has said to you to make sure you have the right end of the stick. You might say to your child, 'So what happened today was . . .' or 'You're feeling cross, then, especially because . . .'

Ask open questions   Gently ask, 'How did you feel about that?' or 'What happened before you hit him?' You will help more using this approach than by closed questioning or using the challenging effect of 'Why?' questions, which tend to be met with 'because . . .' justifications.

Cuddle children if this helps   Some distress experienced by children is best helped by your willingness to listen and to cuddle them close to you. Cuddling does not make the problem go away, of course, but your child may find it easier to bear.

Help your child to consider other perspectives   Good counsellors do not charge in insisting that the person with the problem should look at it all from another, more correct angle. They do, however, encourage other ways of looking at an issue. By adopting this approach, you would be trying to get your child to see a bigger picture, but are not saying that she is wrong. It might help to take a moment to look at the situation from another person's viewpoint, 'Have you thought that Anouska might be hurt by what happened too?' Or you might put some basic psychology to your child, 'You know, I think Jerome must feel very unsure of himself to believe that he has to beat people up to get an invitation to a party.' Other perspectives do not automatically lead to a solution, but they help children to take a broad look at problems with other people. It can help to realise that they are not alone in having strong feelings or experiencing difficulties.

Talk over several possibilities of what to do   Effective counsellors neither lift a solution from a magic bag nor do they let their clients leap at the first solution that comes to mind. Children, even more than adults, sometimes do not consider that they might be able to act to change the situation. Realistically, so much in their young lives is determined by other people that it may not have occurred to them that, in this instance, they could take control.

Sit down with your child, and mull over different possibilities of what could be done. Many problems do not have solutions that make everything suddenly all right. Much of life for adults and children involves resolving difficulties in a way that enables you to cope. Some problems are resolved by thinking of a way to live with the continuing difficulty that feels acceptable to your child.

Consider the following with your child:

- What are the possible ways of tackling this problem? Your child may have some ideas, and you can add some, but your ideas should have the same weight as your child's.
- Out of the possibilities (which may not be many), which one does your child find more acceptable? What is she happier to try?
- Encourage your child to concentrate on what could be possible rather than the pessimistic 'It'll never work'.
- Agree with your child what she will do and when.

• Sometimes your child may like to practise on you what will be said or how she will act.

Follow up the conversation later   Ask your child later how things went. Be pleased with your child if she has resolved a problem successfully, stress that 'You did it not me.' You want children to gain confidence in their ability to resolve problems themselves so that, although you are there to help through conversation, they are the ones to actually solve it. It is this experience that will help your child directly the next time there is a problem, not the belief that you are the font of all wisdom.

If they want, talk through with them to what extent they have not resolved the problem. Be ready, if appropriate, to add your adult input directly, but stress to children that this is another step to help make their best better. They have not failed.

Seek further help if necessary   Sometimes you, as a parent, may be too close to offer the full help that your child needs. You may have to consider seeking some professional counselling for your child, and possibly for yourself too. This is often the case when you are overwhelmed by the loss of someone through death or the pain of divorce. We give some general guidance on professionals who may help in the Resources section.

Final thoughts

Ideally, communication in the family should be enjoyable most of the time. It is all about chatting on the way back from school or over mealtimes; talking as you do something together or while you're busy with household tasks which use your hands, but not all of your brain. Have a two-way exchange of ideas, views and experiences. It will not be successful, however, if exchanges are scheduled in like a dental appointment.

Every parent needs to pay proper attention to what their children are saying. This means looking as well as listening. Children can be tolerant of your not looking if there is a good reason, such as you are cooking or driving, so long as you reassure them 'I am listening' and your replies demonstrate that you are. It's not fair to expect your children to listen properly to you, unless you, in turn, listen to them by giving them your full attention. Nor will they be impressed if you show that you think it is quite all right to interrupt them, but if they do the interrupting, you get angry.

Obviously, it is useful for you to know what is going on in your child's life in the hours they are at school. The habit of chatting with your children makes it more likely that they will tell you if something is bothering them or if they are confused. This has to be the first step in any attempt to help as a good parent to your child. Often there will be no problem and you will simply enjoy conversations with your children and they with you.

CHAPTER FIVE

Growing up

Between the ages of five and eleven, your children will be moving away from you in some ways, as they start to have activities without you. As hard as it is for most parents, you need to look towards teaching them all you can so that they are able, in the end, to take good care of themselves when you are not there to help directly.

You can teach children within this age group a great deal, and you have a chance to do it in a relaxed way. You can pass on some of the skills you have learned in your adult life, and can start the process *now*, before it is crucial that your children can feed themselves on a small budget or iron their own clothes.

Teaching independence

Teaching children to be independent is a long-term project. It's a gradual process and so need not be painful for you or your children. However, it will not happen effectively if you wait until you are so fed up with doing everything for your children that you shout at them to get off their backsides and do something.

This age group can be asked, encouraged, taught and cajoled to take on some responsibility for themselves. When they were younger than five, the issue was usually 'Can they do this?', as with so many physical skills, they did not have the coordination. With the five to elevens, the questions steadily become 'Are they willing to do it?' and 'Can I trust them on their own?'

Your children will not learn to go it alone in one giant leap. Some things they may learn quite quickly, but many others will take time and repetition. It is neither necessary nor wise to move from watching them like a hawk in the kitchen straight to handing over the chip pan and leaving them to get on with it. You could think of the process as moving, with your child, through the following stages:

1 You do something entirely for your child – either because she cannot do it, or you judge it is not yet safe for her to do so, however much she may want to.
2 You encourage him to join in and to do a bit of it, but you are still basically in charge. He helps you cook, you show him how the controls work, but you do not leave him alone for a moment.
3 You say 'Go on you try it', and are ready beside your child to help if needed and to check her achievement at the end.
4 You let your child get on with it alone, but you tend to check that everything has gone smoothly, being ready with encouragement, feedback and additional help if needed.
5 You let your child get on with a task, without any supervision and with little or no checking afterwards; not forgetting to say sometimes how impressed you are by what your child can manage all by himself.

How quickly and how far you and your child progress will vary according to the different elements of their growing independence – from keeping themselves clean, to road safety; from managing their own money, to cooking the family dinner.

The following checklist may be useful to see where you are now with your child on a range of everyday activities. Never undervalue the importance of your teaching your children literally how to run an adult life in all the mundane details.

Assessing your child's independence

Place a tick in the column which best represents where you are now with your child on each of the activities below.

- Column 1 means: I'm teaching this to my child at the moment.
- Column 2 means: My child does this now without help or supervision.
- Column 3 should be used for your estimate of when you will start teaching your child this.

ACTIVITY	1	2	3
Crossing the road			
Going to the local shop			
Taking a bath alone			
Washing hair			
Cleaning teeth			
Making a packed lunch			
Choosing what to wear			
Making snacks			
Proper cooking			
Washing up			
Laying the table			
Changing a light bulb or plug			
Operating machines (e.g. washing machine)			
Painting and decorating			
Posting letters			
Ironing			
Mending clothes			
Tidying up			
Polishing and dusting			
Washing the car			

ACTIVITY	1	2	3
Answering the telephone			
Writing off for offers			
Taking care of the pets			
Doing the talking at the dentist or doctor			
Riding a bike on the road			
Anything else?			

Questions

• Where are you in each of these?
• Is it time to move on to encouraging your child to try more for herself?
• Is it time to trust your child alone, or are you expecting too much of him in some things?
• All these things will have to happen some time. If not now, then when?

You may like to check with other parents with children of the same age to see if they are roughly at the same place as you. Your children may be more independent than theirs in some ways and less in others.

Learning by helping out

Children usually like to help out, and can learn a lot in this way. Sometimes children are simply fascinated to watch you. You will encourage your children if you:

• Say 'yes' to their offers of help a lot more often than you say 'no'.
• Find part of the job that your child can manage. Your son may be too short to hang out the washing, but he will be able to

give you the pegs and to decide what you hang up next.

- Encourage rather than criticise. Part of learning will include pointing out how to do something. Try to avoid harping on about things your child cannot do or which she does wrong. Be encouraging, even when you are explaining about mistakes, for example, 'Mainly this is a great weeding job – the only thing is, I want you to look out for these plants next time, because they aren't weeds.'

- Explain what you will be doing, and how and why you do it this way. Some tasks need little explanation, but others need to follow a particular order, either to ensure that the job is carried out properly, or for safety reasons. You know this, but your child does not. So if you have stopped reading instructions, do start again, to emphasise to your child how you learned in the first place.

- Allow more time for doing household tasks when your children help. Do be grateful for what they have done, even if you have to redo it later.

- Praise their efforts and be patient. It will take a while for your children to become competent at certain tasks, so ask yourself 'Is this task done adequately?' – not as well as you – but adequately. If so, compliment your child and let him achieve your standards in time. If the shirt or blouse has to be ironed perfectly, do it yourself and give him the tea towels or clothes that matter less.

- Find them a task while you do your adult job. Sometimes you may have to turn down children's help for reasons of speed, or the nature of what you are doing. If what you are cooking has to be absolutely right, can your child sit and chat with you or read to you? If the DIY task is too risky to give to a child or has to be very accurate, can your child help you plan or design, hand you tools, or get refreshments?

- Deal sympathetically with disasters. However careful you are in teaching them and keeping them safe, at some point your children will make a major mess. This is not necessarily going to be because they were careless or did it deliberately. They may have lost control of something too heavy for them; or they may have tried to use their initiative but it backfired. Find out how it went wrong, explain the lessons to them and if at all possible, clear it up together. They are likely to be upset, so tell them about a similar experience you had as a child. If you can make your children feel better about the disaster, they will learn from the experience.

Overall, do encourage your children to join you in what you are doing. It will be one of the most straightforward ways to pass on your adult skills.

The three Rs and everyday learning

You may underestimate just how much children can learn while they help out, in what seems to you a very mundane domestic job. They learn independence and satisfaction in their growing skills. However, there is also plenty of opportunity for children to practise basic skills of reading, writing and maths. Here are two checklists to get your ideas flowing.

Practising reading and writing

- What you do together often shows your child that you read and write. You can point out that writing is all around your home and on trips out – not just in books. It is on: newspapers or magazines you check for the weather or television programmes; packets of food (labels and ingredients); instructions you read on boxes; local road signs and shop fronts; shopping lists; the summary of the plot on a video; recipes that you can read with your children, even if you now know them by heart; reminder notes to yourself, notes to cancel milk.
- Much of everyday fact finding depends on knowing the alphabet. You can show this to your children as you use:

telephone directories; library book filing systems; dictionaries; indexes to any book; the family address book.

- You can encourage your children to write for simple family needs, initially without making too big a deal about spelling. This may be: a shopping list or adding items to yours, perhaps the flavoured crisps that they love; reminder notes for you, or for themselves for games kit or money for the school trip; their own lists of what they would like for presents; plans, such as what they would like to do over the school holidays; simple letters and postcards; sending off for offers on packets or material from children's television programmes; invitations to parties.

- Keeping an address book. Seven-year-olds and over will soon be ready to have an address book and take responsibility for getting and recording their friends' addresses and telephone numbers. The risk here is of encouraging them to phone their friends at length, so you need to set firm rules to keep expenses under control.

- Keeping a diary. By the age of eight, or earlier, some children like to keep a diary. They may write their private thoughts or use the diary to note events and appointments or birthdays.

Everyday maths

Simple mathematics come up each day, probably more often than you realise. Letting your children help and have a go will help them practise. You will also get clues as to what they can and can't yet manage.

- Planning meals and laying tables. These need attention to 'How many people will be eating?' so 'How many plates do we need?' or 'How much rice/how many potatoes do we need to cook?'

- Cooking involves measuring out and counting. As well as measuring the ingredients, there is also how long it takes to cook something. With a large piece of meat or fish you need to work out time per pound/kilo by actual weight.
- Sharing out food, especially favourite items, uses fractions to keep the peace. 'There are four of you, so you can have exactly a quarter each.'
- To make things – whether household DIY or craft hobbies – children will need the skills of measuring, counting and simple maths. (These activities are also mentioned in Chapter 9.)
- Money is a practical opportunity for applied maths. Children learn about money by: working out what they can buy with their pocket money; buying things with you in a shop, and working out how much four of something at 20p each will cost; children often love poring over toy catalogues – get them to add up how much all their potential purchases will cost. (We return to money matters in Chapter 6.)

What time is it?

A number of parents have found to their amazement, their eight- or nine-year-olds cannot tell the time, even when a year or so ago, they were completing worksheets at school with little problem. If your child has not practised this skill, it may have faded.

Nowadays there are different ways of telling the time: *analogue time* – using clocks or watches with moving 'hands'; or *digital time* – using numbers, which may be on a twelve or twenty-four hour basis. Your child may be confused on some or all of these. You may need to sit down over a number of sessions, and actually teach your child how to tell the time in these different ways. In teaching analogue time it is very useful to have a cardboard pretend clock with moving hands. You can teach digital time from any watches or clocks that you have in your home. Take regular opportunities to get your child to tell you the time and help him sort out any remaining confusions. Telling the time is a complicated skill – don't expect your children to grasp it in one sitting.

Taking care of themselves

Learning to cook

Do teach your children to cook, the boys as well as the girls. They will need to be able to do this in the future, as living from convenience foods is expensive and may result in an unbalanced diet.

First of all, you can show them how to make snacks. They can learn to make their own packed lunches for school or help you to prepare a picnic. You can make impressive eats without cooking. For example, Jane Asher's *Quick party cakes* (Walker Books, 1988) shows how to put together creative cakes with bought ingredients. With your help, children will enjoy making and cooking simple cakes or biscuits and, from time to time, treats like making toffee. **NB** Do remember to teach them how to keep safe in the kitchen at the same time.

You won't manage to help your children if you are in a rush, so try making a cooking session something that you do together on wet weekends. The day will then arrive when your children will be a genuine help when you are short of time. You may have lots of your own favourite recipes to share with your children, but if you are looking for more ideas, we have enjoyed using Fay Maschler's *Teach your child to cook* (Bloomsbury, 1988). She has laid the book out so that learning a basic technique, like how to make a batter, leads straight into using this skill for real meals. There are recipes from a range of cultures and cooking traditions.

Physical care

Your children will not enjoy their childhood if they are expected to keep perpetually clean and neat. However, if you keep to realistic goals, it is possible to encourage your children to begin to take over their own physical care. They may be flattered that you are trusting them.

Keeping healthy

You can look to handing over, steadily, the responsibility for their general hygiene such as hand washing and bathing, washing their hair and cleaning teeth. You have had to do all these for so long, it is easy to overlook the time when your children could, and probably want, to do it for themselves. You will need to do a bit of surreptitious checking for a while as well as reminding them.

You also need to teach your children how to deal with specific health problems that they face. Perhaps they can help with their skin care, if they need to apply special cream, or if your child is prone to nose bleeds or has asthma attacks, he needs to know how to handle the situation when it arises. If your child has a debilitating condition like sickle cell anaemia, she needs to learn how to recognise the signs of an impending crisis.

For your information

There are a number of books for children which explain health and physical care in straightforward language. For the under eights, try Claire Rayner's The body book (Piccolo, 1978), and The getting better book (Piccolo, 1985). Older children need a different style of book. You could try The young scientist book of the human body by Susan Meredith and others (Usborne, 1983).

Going to the toilet

When they were younger, your energy went on getting your children toilet trained and dealing with the inevitable accidents. However, the majority of five-year-olds have full control of their bladder and bowels by day and night, although there will be exceptional accidents, when your child tries to hang on far too long. Also, if children get bad diarrhoea, they may lose control, which will distress them. (Otherwise, if your five-year-old is not toilet-trained during the daytime, it's definitely time to see your doctor. He or she may refer you on to a special clinic. The fact that such clinics exist will tell you that you are not alone. It is, of course, a different matter if your child has a disabling condition that makes it impossible for him to gain control.)

An organisation called ERIC (address follows) estimates that over half a million children in Britain between the ages of six and sixteen still wet their beds at night. If your child does this only very occasionally, you may be prepared to live with it. However, your child may resist accepting overnight stays at friends' houses as he gets older and a school trip lasting over several days will be a serious worry.

For your information

ERIC (Enuresis Resource and Information Centre) is a national centre offering information and advice to parents and professionals alike on the problem of bed wetting. They have practical leaflets aimed at parents and children. Contact them at 65 St Michael's Hill, Bristol BS2 8DZ. Tel: 0272 264920.

First-aid and medicines

Teach your children simple first-aid. Those aged between five and eleven can learn basic procedures like how to clean a cut, get a splinter out, and the importance of putting a burn under cold running water as quickly as possible. If your children love impressive plasters, you will need to get across to them that some grazes and bangs heal better uncovered. Show them what to put on cuts and grazes, including the need to dilute some liquid antiseptics. If you do not show them, enterprising children will soon use their initiative and may get it wrong.

Children can learn responsible use of medicines, including realising that you don't run to the bottle or packet at the first sniffle. Some ailments will clear themselves up. Some do not need medication unless they are causing discomfort or fever. The younger end of this age group still need to be kept well clear of the medicine cabinet, but, as they get older:

- Get into the habit of reading the instructions on bottles and packets with your children.
- Show them how to take a correct dose of something like cough medicine.
- Remind them that some medicines have to be shaken first.
- Make clear which medicines are for external application only, and those which can be taken internally. It is much better to have children too aware of the dangers of poisons than the reverse.

Stress the contents of the cabinet that they are allowed to use, or simply keep these separate from more powerful mixtures.

For your information

You may like to get a straightforward book on common ailments and possible medicines for treatment. The best we have found is Mike Smith's *Handbook of over-the-counter medicines* (Kyle Cathie, 1992).

Dressing and clothes

During the primary school years the headaches over dressing are caused by children not getting dressed in time and by arguments over what your children want to wear. If your children have a school uniform, then the discussions on school days will focus on whether they have a cleanish version of everything to wear. If they have a choice of apparel, discussions or arguments are likely.

GROWING UP

If your child is a slow dresser, the options are to nag, to do it for him, or to get your child up earlier. Getting him up earlier may help if your child genuinely needs more time. Nagging makes for miserable mornings. If your child is something of a dreamer who loses track of time, then you may need to experiment with something such as a five minute sand timer, and get her to dress against the timer or two turns of it.

Many parents are not at their best in the morning, so it's not a good time for arguments about what will be worn today – 'No, I've said before, you can't wear your Batman costume to school.' It can be less stressful to take time the previous night to lay out the approved set of clothes with your child, and stick to it the next morning. Once you have a set of family rules about suitable clothes for the time of year and for school, then it is only fair to give your child the final choice of exactly what to wear. Clashing colours and totally different patterns may not be your preference, but does it really matter, right at this moment? You may wish to tackle style as a separate issue.

Some five-year-olds already have strong preferences for certain clothes, but between the ages of five and eleven, most children will develop definite opinions as to what kinds of clothes they prefer to wear – which may or may not be in line with fashion! Children may look to you for a source of style which is quite flattering: 'I want proper pants like Daddy's' or 'You wear pretty petticoats, can I have one like that?' Often when parents are fashion-conscious, children follow suit. Occasionally children will actually walk off with your clothes. You have the right to say 'No' to this. With the under-eights, you will probably be preventing them routing through your cupboards for dressing up clothes. As the teenage years approach, your clothes may be under threat for actual outside wear. One father we know only realised his daughters were borrowing his jumpers when work colleagues started commenting on his perfume.

Stronger pressure will come from friends, particularly as your children approach the fashion-conscious teens. Throughout, parents need to blend what is sensible with what is fashionable.

These are not mutually exclusive, particularly if you agree an overall approach with your offspring and buy clothes together. Unfortunately, fashion and clothes can become an issue, more often regarding cost than taste. We return to this in Chapter 6.

Growing up physically

Physical changes

In the first five years, children change dramatically in size and looks. They are still growing and changing between the ages of five and eleven, but the pace has slowed. Now the different parts of their bodies are getting closer to the adult proportions. For example, by the age of eight, a child's head is ninety per cent of the adult size. It is not necessary to keep weighing your children or measuring their height, but you would expect them to grow out of clothes from time to time, either upwards or outwards. Start worrying if your child is losing weight with no obvious reason, such as a serious illness. If your child remains noticeably overweight compared with friends of the same age, then it would be wise to get some advice. Start with your doctor.

Another aspect of physical change is when they get their second set of teeth. The age when they first lose a baby tooth is very variable. Some children start as early as five; some may be as late as seven. Your dentist will let you know if there is any reason to worry.

Puberty

A few boys and girls begin some of the changes of puberty as early as ten years old. Regardless of whether your child is an early or late developer, you both need to know what is coming. Your children may already have asked you questions about babies. However, these conversations will not necessarily have led to practical details of how girls develop into women and boys into men. Bear in mind that the age at which change begins is precisely that – just the beginning. Some aspects of physical development will happen very gradually, and it may be a while before you or your child notices anything. For example, the development of breasts in girls and changes in the penis and testicles of a boy are very gradual. However, the start of periods for a girl and voice change in a boy are more obvious.

As you will no doubt remember, some of the most awkward parts of puberty are not the physical changes, but how you feel about what's happening. If your children start puberty earlier than average, then they may have few, if any, friends who are also experiencing the changes. They may need your emotional support and perhaps a discreet reminder to other adults that, although your son is tall, he is still only eleven years old.

Parents are sometimes more careful to talk with their daughters about the changes of puberty. Perhaps it is the realisation that periods will certainly arrive at some point, which in turn causes concern about unwanted pregnancies. However, boys can also be very worried by physical changes or by events such as their first wet dream, if they are totally unprepared. To help you discuss these changes with your children, you will find plenty of useful material in *You and your adolescent – a parent's guide for ages 10–20* by Laurence Steinberg (Vermilion, 1992). There are some good books around for girls in particular. Our daughter recommends *Have you started yet?* by Ruth Thomson (Pan, 1980).

Sex education

Some form of sex education will be part of the curriculum once your children enter secondary school. At the primary level, it is the decision of the school governing body whether to introduce a programme for children. Some parents leave all aspects of sex education to schools. We feel that this is a great pity.

Do make every effort to talk with your children about this side to growing up as well as all the other changes. Unless you chat with your children, they may come to completely the wrong con-clusions. It is not unusual, for example, for nine- or ten-year-olds to conclude that their parents have only had sex as many times as there are children in the family. Unless you have opened up the topic, they are also very unlikely to come to you with questions or worries later.

For your information

The Family Planning Association has a very practical set of booklets, *The Growing Up* series. The first one addresses how to answer your children's questions. Contact the FPA for details at 27–35 Mortimer Street, London W1N 7RJ. Tel: 071 636 7866.

There are some good books available on babies and childbirth. These vary in the level of explanation and the explicitness of the photographs. You might want to check on the content before you buy or borrow, if only to prepare yourself for the questions your child may ask. We like Camilla Jessel's *The joy of birth – a book for families to share* (Methuen, 1982). Also, Sheila Kitzinger's *Being born* (Dorling Kindersley, 1986) has wonderful photographs of developing babies before birth.

Part of sex education will be communicating values to children and teenagers about considerate and safe behaviour towards others. Schools are expected to address moral issues as well as the mech-anics of sex. As parents you have the right and responsibility to put your values to your children. Be ready to explain to them your reasons for what you believe.

Final thoughts

It is only fair that children should steadily help around the house and take responsibility for their own things. If you have a large family, it may be crucial that all the children pitch in with the household tasks. What you want to avoid, however, is your children taking on adult worries, or feeling the burden of responsibility for you or for brothers or sisters. As a parent, you are trying to encourage your children to learn the skills and the approaches that will help them as teenagers and adults. As you see your children becoming competent, you will be more confident of their ability to handle life's decisions. This gradual hand-over will also help to provide a firm foundation for a happy relationship when your children become adults too.

Part of the process of helping your children towards independence is accepting that they are growing up physically. Try to find at least one person in the family who can feel comfortable talking about this topic. During the five to elevens, and on into the teenage years, your children are also developing emotionally and they can and will challenge you very fiercely on occasion. Sometimes it helps to enjoy the funny side of this together. Our own children recommend the following books as an amusing insight into parent—child relationships: *I was a teenage worrier* by Ros Asquith (Picadilly Press, 1992); *Not dressed like that you don't!* and the sequel, *Everybody else does! Why can't I!* by Yvonne Coppard (Picadilly Press, 1991 & 1992); *Coping with parents* by Peter Corey (Hippo, 1989); and Jim and Duncan Eldridge, *The complete how to handle grown-ups* (Red Fox, 1991).

CHAPTER SIX

Money matters

Learning about money is a crucial part of what children need to learn before the teenage years. It is a good idea to start now.

Handling money

You do not wish your children to be burdened by your money worries, but they do need to understand that you don't have limitless funds and that they have to make some choices. For special occasions you may be prepared to buy your children whatever they want, so long as it falls within an agreed budget limit. By all means show them an electricity bill and tell them that this is only part of what you pay out each month. You could use this in support of a campaign for lights to be switched off when nobody is in the room.

Children's own money

In dealing with money, your children will show a combination of your style and their own personality. Money may burn a hole in your pocket, yet your child may be a born saver. You need to be consistent over issues of what is your money and what is theirs.

For example, with some children, parents swiftly have to develop a strategy on borrowing against future pocket money.

Saving

If your children are capable of saving, or relatives give them large sums, then you need to decide where to put it and how easy to make the access. As of April 1991, you can register children's accounts with banks and building societies to have interest paid gross, that is without income tax deducted. There are exceptions to this, however, specifically designed to stop you escaping tax by pretending your money belongs to your children. Inland Revenue leaflet IR110 explains the procedure.

Choosing how to spend money

There is no reason for children to make what parents would consider to be sensible choices about how they spend their money. Your children probably think you make some pretty weird choices in how you spend your money.

There are two sides to this. First, it is fair in principle that children should spend their own money however they choose. This is also a good guideline to adopt during the teenage years, if your offspring earn money from a weekend job. (Obviously, at some point in the future, you can reasonably expect them to make a contribution to the household expenses.) Second, whilst children are your responsibility, you may wish to place limits on the principle of 'spend your own money how you like'. You may well say an absolute 'No' to an air rifle or to a pet snake. You may put a limit on the number of sweets, especially if you have firm rules about when these can be eaten. Thereafter, if the chocolate bar they buy is revolting, then they have to live with their choice. If they wish they had not blown all their pocket money on yet another plastic figure, then that unfortunately is life.

Value for money

Children are more likely to learn the value of money and of a considered decision if you let them make some mistakes. If you attempt to control their spending totally, then they will learn little except to get angry with you. Encourage your children to look for value for money and to compare prices in different shops. You can say you don't think that the currently advertised collectable is good value. However, if that is how they wish to spend their money – fair enough.

Earning money

Your five- to eleven-year-olds cannot have jobs as such – it is illegal to employ children under the age of thirteen except under special circumstances. The law restricts the hours of the over-thirteens and sets out firm limits to the conditions for younger children who work as actors or models.

However, as far as pocket money is concerned, you will have to decide in your family whether it is a right, or a privilege earned through doing household tasks. It is possible to compromise, by having a fixed amount that is delivered regardless, and carefully negotiating any extra for specific tasks, say, tidying up their room by Saturday lunchtime without your having to nag.

It can be pleasant for children to earn small amounts by pitching in on tasks that you would not normally expect them to do, such as weeding the garden. You will realise from Chapter 3, however, that we don't think it's wise to allow your child to demand payment for tasks that are part of being a member of the household.

Money and shops

The five to elevens sometimes have a rather magical view of money. It comes from their limited understanding of how money works. You can help your children, by teaching them that:

- you buy things in shops with money;

- cheques are like money;
- credit card purchases have to be paid for in the end;
- many people put their everyday money into banks or building societies for safe-keeping; and
- hole-in-the-wall cash dispensers usually only work if you have money in your account.

Buying in shops

You can encourage your children to do their own buying in shops, staying near them until they feel confident. There are many parts to 'buying' including:

- reading the price;
- understanding what this means in coins and notes;
- working out if you have enough money to buy the chosen item;
- finding where to pay and waiting;
- getting attention in a queue, which is unfairly difficult some-times for children;
- getting the money ready;
- paying for things before you leave the store and before you eat, unwrap or play with them;
- waiting for, receiving and checking change; and
- holding on to a receipt if you stay in the store afterwards.

Consumer rights

Just because the purchase is a toy, doesn't mean that children have to suffer if it doesn't work. You may need to explain to your children that they have a right to return faulty purchases to the shop for a refund or an exchange. This justifies why it is worth their keeping the receipt for a little while. You can help your child to gain confidence in returning defective toys by doing the talking yourself on the first occasion. You need to do this assertively, that is with firm-ness and courtesy, and persist if the shop staff are unhelpful. Your child will then copy your style, with your encouragement. If you personally find this difficult, take the opportunity to crank up your ability to be assertive and not aggressive on behalf of your children. You may find it easier to make the effort on their behalf rather than for yourself. If your children hear you apologising unnecessarily or getting angry quickly, they will copy your behaviour.

> **For your information**
>
> Either of the following books could help you to become more assertive as an adult. Despite their titles, they are relevant to home as well as work and to men as well as women. *Assertiveness at work* by Ken Back and Kate Back (McGraw-Hill, 1991); and *A woman in your own right* by Anne Dickson (Quartet Books, 1984).

Children spending your money

It is wise to establish that, whatever your circumstances, you are not prepared to buy everything that your children want. You will have to stand firm against serious whining on more than one occasion. Give your reason for refusing and then keep repeating your 'No'. When you've really had enough, don't answer the cries of 'But I need it'.

At some point you will face the pleading of 'Everybody else has one!' You need to be strong and see where the pressures are going. When they were younger, they nagged for toys. Soon, if not already, it will be a games computer and endless new games. Lying ahead will be expensive bikes and designer clothes.

A marketing ploy that really started in the 1980s is the enormous range of plastic collectables, often linked with a television series. The range is then soon updated with new versions. Children compare their holdings with those of their friends and can mount serious pressure of 'I must have . . .' In a year or so, many of these crucial possessions will be at the back of the cupboard, forgotten. The pressure on you as a parent is real, and the pressure on your child from their friends may be high. You need to deal with this by being prepared to say 'No' and stick to this decision when your child wants you to pay out at random. You can work to alert your children to the pressures of advertising, but they won't remain untouched.

If your children don't have pocket money, consider starting now. They need the first-hand experience of managing money. They have to decide what matters most for spending their money, rather than nagging you for yours. If they want something that badly, then they can save up for it.

Fashion, clothes and money

It is neither worrying nor surprising that children should care about how they look. They will have likes and dislikes over clothes and prefer to wear the kinds of clothes that their friends are wearing. However, it is worrying if children are convinced that they are a nobody without the correct clothes and parents feel pressured into regularly buying expensive clothes.

Likes and dislikes in clothes

Some parents realise long before their children are five that it is risky to buy clothes without their children being present. These parents offer a choice with boundaries set by a price range, number of items, or use, for example, that their child needs a warm coat. This is a sensible idea. Both children and adults feel happier or more comfortable in what they feel suits them.

Fashion

Fights over fashion between the generations are not new. Many of today's parents had furious arguments with their own parents about what they could wear or buy. Some will admit to having climbed out of the home via the drain pipe to sneak off in forbidden clothes, or leaving the house in a long coat to disguise what was underneath.

What is different in the 1990s is how much children, as opposed to young adults, are now getting caught up in the conviction that they are worthless individuals if they don't match the current street fashion. They want the right label, made as large as possible so other people can see it. With this comes the conviction, not a new one, that more expensive clothes must be better than a cheaper range. The fashion industry, with the accompanying advertising, has created or at least latched onto this new market. The 1990s leisure look is not cheap and, as usual in the fashion world, the aim is to change what is correct dress regularly. As a result, your older child will inform you that the trainers or jeans that were fine two months ago are seriously embarrassing to be seen in now. There are a number of different approaches you could take to deal with the fashion arguments:

- *Approach 1: Buy whatever clothes your child wants*   If you have plenty of spare money and like clothes yourself, why not? You may like to see your child dressed fashionably yourself.

  If you do use this approach, you will need to raise the following with your children: Although you are happy to splash out on clothes, you are not a bottomless source of money for everything; and what makes your child likable and acceptable is more than the clothes that she or he wears. Clothes are seen as part of our identity, but should not be all of it. Encourage your children to find confidence in what is inside them – what they are, not just how they look. At some point in the future your children will have to fund buying their own clothes, and they need to realise that they may not be able to keep up the flow of new clothes in the same way that you have, without building up large debts.

- *Approach 2: Flatly refuse to buy anything in high fashion for your child*   This may be crucial if you have a very tight budget. You may also decide that you wish to instill your values in your child – ones that oppose slavishly following fashion.

  If you take this line, then it is only fair to offer your children such choice as you can. They have views and you would be most unwise to insist that your child wears your own choice of style in clothing. It is fair that your children should be able to save their own money and spend it on what you might think are stupid clothes.

- *Approach 3: The compromise*   This offers choice within limits. Decide on a reasonable clothes budget for your children, explain to them how much has to be bought, and what is and what is not negotiable. School uniform may be compulsory. Underwear is needed but the style is their choice. Then involve them in choices about how the rest is spent. If they want high fashion clothes, then they may not be able to have many of them. You may put an upper price limit for items like trainers. If they want something very expensive, then they may have to contribute their pocket money or have the item as part of a present.

Pressure from friends

Fashion bullying becomes a problem for some children. They are insulted, ridiculed and even attacked because they have the wrong clothes. This increases the pressure on parents to equip their children in order to protect them. This is not wise. Sadly children can be bullied for something else instead. Bullies can pick on your child's skin colour, being a boy or girl, wearing glasses, supposedly being sissy or posh. The list is endless. You cannot buy your children out of their physical appearance or family background. So it's not useful in the end to feel forced into doing it for clothes just because you can buy these. If your children are being bullied, Chapter 8 offers some suggestions.

Final thoughts

During their middle childhood, children need to learn the value and the mechanics of money – what it is, how you get it, what it buys. You need to take an active part rather than wringing your hands and moaning 'Kids! They think money grows on trees!' If you take this attitude, they certainly will think you have an unending supply of it.

Thoroughly nagged parents will sometimes say 'I can't say "No"'. Well, of course, you can, it is just that saying it once isn't always enough. Children will learn that lengthy griping doesn't get them anywhere, but *only* if you hold out. It can be exhausting to convince your children that you aren't a pushover, but who said being a parent was easy? Saying 'No' sometimes doesn't make you a mean person, whatever names your children may call you. Saying 'Yes' to any and every demand for your hard-earned cash does make you a sucker.

CHAPTER SEVEN

Taking care – keeping safe

Most parents would desperately wish to ensure that their children will never come to any harm, never be hurt, even if it is only feelings that are bruised. It is a hard fact to face that you cannot make this a certainty. Indeed, it wouldn't be emotionally healthy to try to cushion your children from all the ups and downs of normal life. Within reason, children's confidence can be boosted by successfully tackling a difficult situation. You can, however, try to teach your children safe ways to behave. This includes sharing with them strategies for dealing with the pressures that other children may put on them. When you have done your level best, then it is a parent's job to be there for them if they are hurt or shaken.

Child Care

Uninformed people talk sometimes as if all your child care problems disappear when your children enter primary school. Of course they don't, because school hours bear little relationship to normal working hours. If you have a paid job, then you will need to arrange for child care, unless you are one of the small number who can tie your hours to the school day and terms. Even then, children get sick and need to be cared for at home.

Who cares for the children?

If you live in Scotland, it is against the law to leave a child under the age of twelve in the house without an older person present. In England and Wales, there is no age that is legally set. However, parents or other carers can be prosecuted for neglect, if a case is made that children were endangered by being left alone.

Even if the law allows you to make your own decision, do consider other alternatives to leaving primary school-age children on their own. Only children can be very lonely or nervous in the house. If you have a larger family, then it is asking a lot of older brothers and sisters to be responsible for younger ones until you come home. Although ten- or eleven-year-olds can be very competent, they may panic if faced with an accident or illness. You may also ruin their social life. If they are invited to a friend's house, they cannot go, unless that family is prepared to have the younger child as well. If you do decide to let your children stay alone in the house on a regular basis, you must take the time to teach them very carefully about personal safety. We return to this later on in the chapter.

If you cannot make child care arrangements between the adults in a family, you have to look outside. Do take as much care in choosing a childminder or an after-school group as you would have done for younger children. Five to elevens are tougher, but they can still be distressed by carers who are unpleasant or by unfriendly groups. Childminders and after-school/holiday groups catering for the under-eights have to be registered with the local social services under the Children Act 1989. There are only a few exceptions to this ruling. If you are able to afford a nanny or au pair, you still need to make your choice of person as carefully as you can. If you share a nanny, and three or more families are involved, that person has to register in the same way as a childminder.

For your information

The following two organisations are concerned about good quality child care for the over-fives: Kids' Club Network, 279–81 Whitechapel Road, London E1 1BY. Tel: 071 247 3009; and National Childminding Association, 8 Masons Hill, Bromley, BR2 9EY. Tel: 081 464 6164/460 5427.

Dangers to health

It is worth your while thinking about certain areas of health care even though they are unlikely to present problems until your children approach the teenage years. It is also worth bearing in mind that you may be pushed into answering questions by what your children hear on television or in the playground. With care and good fortune, your children may not be facing any of the risks mentioned below until they are into teenage years, but it is a possibility, and you should be ready to talk about them. (We return in Chapter 8 to dealing with pressure from friends.)

Alcohol

Young people's attitudes to alcohol are strongly influenced by those of their parents – heavy drinking parents are more likely to have heavy drinking adolescents. Your best bet is to be factual with your children about alcohol. Show them that you neither drink to excess nor use drink as a prop – to calm you down or cheer you up. If you do have a drink problem, seriously consider seeking help now.

Smoking

This is a habit that inevitably affects other people. It not only has a high chance of causing the smoker harm but may well cause harm to non-smokers too through passive smoking. Children often follow in the footsteps of smoking parents.

If you smoke, you will help your child best by giving up. If you find this impossible, at least aim to cut down substantially, or consider smoking only outside the house. If you can, try not to smoke in front of your children. If you do, you might give them the idea that smoking is okay. Take a firm stand against any suggestion that it is part of being grown-up and don't be the one to introduce your children to the habit.

Drugs and solvent abuse

How much you need to say to your children will depend a great deal on the area in which you live. Some families discover to their horror that drug pushers are appearing outside primary schools. It depends also on what is introduced to your child's group. It may need just one child who has tried pills or glue sniffing to encourage the rest.

Whatever is happening locally, your children will almost certainly hear something about drugs and drug abuse through television programmes or by noticing health advertisements. There are several approaches you can adopt, all of which apply equally to tobacco addiction:

- Discuss the issues of drugs as well as other kinds of substance abuse with your children when the topic arises.
- Answer their questions and explain how young people can get involved through feeling unable to say 'No'.
- Explain that the initial good feelings brought on by drugs do not last.
- Find out what you can about warning signs of drug and solvent abuse and be aware if your child seems different.

If you find you are worried, don't automatically jump to conclusions. Do remember that some children get moody and irritable because they are worried or tired; while others become very secretive for periods of time as they plan a surprise or make something. Some children will almost certainly get glue on their clothes while making models or involving themselves in other innocent activities.

As in all aspects of looking after your children, you need to check the information. Don't react in haste before you have the whole picture. However, if you are seriously concerned, then don't let matters drag on.

> **For your information**
>
> If you would like to know more about solvent abuse, try: *Sniffing solutions* edited by Richard Ives, available from the National Children's Bureau, 8 Wakley Street, London EC1V 7QE.

Teaching safe behaviour

Danger and physical activities

Some children seem to be born swinging from vine to vine like mini-Tarzans. Some combine Tarzan with poor judgement and are covered in bruises for much of their childhood. As parents, you walk the line between letting your children try physical activities and preventing them from doing really dangerous things. Although five- and six-year-olds have a much better sense of danger than, say, a three-year-old, it is far from perfect. Their expectation of what might be dangerous will be limited by their experiences so far. It will also be seasoned by their temperament – some children are more wary than others.

You can help five- to eleven-year-olds to become adept at avoiding known dangers by warning them. The difficulty is that they often fail to see that something could go wrong with a new activity that they are planning. They also become increasingly vulnerable to dares from other children. If your child is having trouble with this, you will probably need to talk through some strategies to side-step dangerous challenges.

It may be possible to get together with other parents in the area to exert consistent pressure on all your children. For example, some friends of ours talked with other parents to present a united front on safety gear when skateboarding. One or two children alone would have refused to wear helmets and knee protectors, concerned that they stood out from the rest, but because all the families were in agreement, the safety gear was seen by the children as what any well-dressed skateboarder would wear.

Children need watching and warning. However, keep the list of dangers fairly short, otherwise your children will write you off as an all-round fusspot and ignore every warning you make. It is important that you remain credible to your children, so that they listen to you later on when you try to warn them about potentially lethal risks, like AIDS or drugs. You should try to get across the level of risk involved – the probability of something going wrong. Risk is what might happen, not what will definitely happen. In other words, saying 'Don't bolt your food, you'll choke' is usually unhelpful; lots of people eat in a hurry and don't choke. Likewise lots of people dash across the road and escape being run over. Try to get across to your children that some risks are not worth taking. They may get away with it, but if they don't, then the possible consequences of something like running across the road without looking are very, very serious.

Safety at home

Remember what we said earlier (page 82) about the law and leaving children unattended.

Rules in the house

Practically speaking, many parents have to decide for themselves at what age and for how long they feel it is right to leave their children alone in the house. Basic safety rules are a must. These will include what your child is allowed to do and what they absolutely must not do. For example, your child might know that she can make herself a sandwich but she mustn't use the cooker, if you're not there. The guide below offers some basic tips to rehearse with your children *before* you leave them alone for the first time.

Safety for children at home

Telephone calls and knocks at the door

Some of these will also apply if you are in the house with your child:

- Don't let your children go to the front door alone. If you are in the house, make sure you are there too or have checked who is at the door. If they are alone, they should never open the door, unless it is for a member of the family (grandparent/aunt) or a very good friend.
- Teach your child to answer the telephone with only part of the number or with just 'Hello'. Decide on a phrase for your child to use if he is alone or you are in the bath. This might be, 'Mummy is busy right now, please call back.' Certainly he should not tell an unknown caller that he is alone in the house. If your children are reliable, let them write down a message.
- Teach your child that she doesn't have to answer questions or continue to talk on the telephone. If she is unfortunate enough to get an offensive call, prepare her to lay the phone on one side and leave the creep at the other end with no response and a mounting bill. The phone can be replaced later on.
- Unfortunately some burglars do knock at the door or phone as a means of establishing if the house is empty. This is the reason why a number of books about children's safety advise that you can let your child answer the phone and go to the door, but *not* open it, and shout a message like the phrase we suggested for the telephone.
- Obviously, your children should have a note of your whereabouts – address and telephone number – so they can contact you easily.
- Be sure your children know how to make an emergency call (999) and understand the kind of circumstances in which they should do this.

Personal safety

Parents, and sometimes their children, recognise dangers from two main sources: strangers who might injure or murder children and danger from the roads. It is unnerving to read newspaper reports of children who have been abducted. However, available statistics show that children are far more likely to be injured by a car than harmed by a strange adult. The level of danger from strangers has scarcely risen over twenty years. The sad fact is that children are still far more likely to suffer physical or sexual abuse from within their own families, or from people that they know already, than from strangers.

In the past, parents tended to teach their children the basic rules of 'Don't take sweets from strangers' and 'Don't go with strangers.' Tragically this has not proved to be adequate protection for some children because: (a) a child's mental picture of a stranger is not wholly reliable — a few friendly overtures, an apparently nice appearance, and an unknown or scarcely known adult is no longer seen as a stranger and therefore not covered by the rules; and (b) children can also be put at risk by absolute rules of behaviour — 'Don't be rude to adults', 'Answer adults when they ask you something', 'Don't shout and scream' are all rules that have exceptions, when adults themselves misbehave. Children need more general rules that apply to all adults.

Safety with adults

- Communicate to your child 'Your body belongs to you, you have a right to say "No" '. Children need to feel it is all right to say a firm 'No' to any adult, family or not, who touches them in a way that does not feel right to them. This includes being cuddled or kissed when they do not want to be. Stress that most adults have no business touching or asking to see children's private parts.

  When they are young, you obviously help them wash this area but if they have some problem there, itching for example, it is courteous for a parent or the family doctor to ask a child before taking a look. This prevents children seeing anyone as having the right to see or touch their genitals. Everyone needs the owner's permission.

This personal, assertive, right can also stand your child in good stead if they have to deal with intrusive games at school involving a precocious sexual element. Girls or boys need to feel confident that they can shout 'No' to other children and complain to adults, and that this is not making a fuss about nothing.

- Tell them that if somebody will not take notice of their 'No' then they should tell on them. Children can only protect themselves up to a point. Some adults or much older children will persist with threats or bribes. Children need to feel sure that troubles with an adult or child, even from within the family, can be reported to a parent or other trusted adult without any negative consequences.
- Make it known that they shouldn't keep a secret that doesn't feel right. Most adults who abuse children are known to them. So, these adults depend on entwining the child in secrecy. It is simpler to have a family rule that 'we don't have secrets'. People within a family should be able to trust each other and share things that don't feel right, without fear of recrimination. Pleasant things like keeping quiet about what you have bought Daddy for his birthday can be called surprises.
- Adults have to keep to the rules too. Children need to be reassured that it is not their responsibility to sort out the nice adults from the nasty ones. It is adults who have the responsibility to behave properly. If they do not behave properly, then the usual politeness rules to adults are suspended.

Help your children to focus on adults' behaviour. Sensible adults do not strike up conversations with children they do not know, especially if those children are on their own. No adult should invite children for a ride in their car or into their house without their parents' knowledge, even if those adults are known slightly. Unknown or scarcely known adults should not ask children to help them; whether this is with directions, finding lost dogs or anything else.

Children have the right to feel suspicious about any adult who acts in this way. You must support your children in how they have acted, even if you are sure, in the end, that the man from the end of your road or the woman from the sweet shop meant no harm.

- Teach your children the basics of personal safety. Beginning with the above examples, talk over with your children what is 'odd' behaviour which should not be trusted. Teach your children that if they are faced with odd behaviour or any adult who tries to grab them, they should shout as loud as they can and run towards a house or into a shop. Teach them not to approach a suspect adult but to keep two-arms length distance and get away – fast.

Keep dangers in perspective

You don't want your children totally unnerved, believing that dangerous adults are lurking around every corner. Teach personal safety much like road safety – as a pattern of sensible behaviour that children must know in case of trouble. You can stress to your children that the vast majority of adults are kindly towards children and mean them no harm at all.

You can show your children how a sensible adult should behave by what you do. For example, don't start conversations with children you don't know, offer them sweets or pick them up. If your children's friends turn up at the door, asking to come in and play, then get them to telephone home from your house to tell their parents where they are. This supposes, of course, that it is convenient for them to come in to play. If you see unknown children who appear lost or distressed, help them by accompanying them to somewhere public, where you and they can be spotted by the adult who has lost them or can call for assistance.

Don't let the recent publicity about damage to children from strangers and sexual abuse shake your judgement about normal affectionate behaviour in your family. Of course it's fine to cuddle your children as much as you can and they want. Touch them comfortably. Let them know what happy physical contact is like.

If your children do have an unpleasant or frightening experience, they will need your support and lots of your time. As hard as it may be for you as a parent, it will be important for your child to be able to talk about what has happened. She will need desperately to know that her feelings are taken seriously, and will need to be reassured, maybe again and again, that nobody is blaming her. As you teach personal safety, be careful to avoid any impression that the responsibility is all theirs. Sometimes the odds against them will be too strong for them to take care of themselves.

For more information

Try the organisation *Kidscape*, which has practical material on teaching children personal safety. Contact them at: World Trade Centre, Europe House, London E1 9AA. Tel: 071 488 2400.

Road safety

A shockingly high number of children are killed or injured on the roads each year. However, this is not keeping pace, in statistical terms, with the rise in the amount of traffic over the last twenty years. What seems to be happening is that parents are protecting their children by keeping them off the roads. The primary school children of the 1990s are not allowed to take themselves to school or cycle around like previous generations.

It is understandable that parents ferry their five to elevens around quite a bit. However, you won't be able to do this for ever. Now is the time to be teaching your children safe behaviour on the roads and how to travel independently. Show them all this whilst you are still accompanying them. You will have to let them go at some point in the future. Get them ready. It may help if you look back now at the five steps we laid out in Chapter 5 when we were talking about teaching children to be independent.

The elements of road safety

As pedestrians, your children need to learn the following:

- Pick a safe place to cross the road, preferably at a marked crossing.
- Avoid coming out between parked cars, but if there is no choice, emerge carefully to the edge of the cars until you can see.
- Never, never rush out. This is especially dangerous when you are shorter than your surroundings.
- Unless you are crossing at exactly the same time as someone else, don't assume that the road is still clear a few seconds later. This is a danger when children run to join an adult who is already halfway across a road.
- Stand where you can see the traffic and it can see you. Look right, left and right again. Listen for traffic you can't see. If it looks safe to cross, walk briskly, preferably not running. Keep looking and listening whilst you cross.
- Avoid crossing on corners or bends. If you can't see what is coming, traffic can't see you.
- If in doubt, don't cross.

Stress to your children that all this still applies when roller skating, skateboarding or riding a bicycle on the pavement.

As cyclists on the road, your children need to learn the following:

- As a road user you have to obey the rules of the road. This includes traffic lights, one-way streets, everything. This point seems to escape a number of adult cyclists.
- Check regularly on the state of your bike, including testing the brakes. Don't borrow friends' bikes without checking their brakes first.

- Wear a proper cyclist's helmet. This will offer some protection to the most vulnerable part of the body in an accident.
- It is very risky to show off when cycling. This includes racing, sudden and unsignalled turns and messing about in the road.

Your adult responsibility is to wear a helmet yourself if you cycle. Do watch out for children as pedestrians and cyclists. When you take evasive action whilst driving with your children in the car, point out to them what has happened and why.

It is the law that anyone, of whatever age, travelling in the front of a car must be restrained appropriately. If rear seat belts are fitted, or your car was manufactured from 1987 on, it is now a legal requirement for passengers in the back to wear those belts. Do fit rear seat belts if you don't have them, as their use dramatically reduces the risk of injury or death to children travelling in the back seat.

On the move – letting your children go

Between their fifth and eleventh birthday, you will gradually need to let your children do more things on their own. This is a complex decision which involves weighing up your children's temperaments, where you live and the activity that they wish to do. Your first concern, as parents, is for your children's safety.

Ground rules for trips

A lot of 'letting go' depends on your child's individual competence and your confidence. Of course, there are steps in loosening your careful watch over your children. You can stagger the kinds of activity that you let them do and when. A good move is to establish some ground rules with your children. These apply whether they are with you or are venturing out on short trips without you. Take a look at the guide.

Ground rules for trips

Establish a set of rules with your children that you expect to be followed. Ground rules and related skills can include:

- Where you meet within a shop or shopping centre if you get separated or you have given the go-ahead for your child to wander a little.
- How to find the main desk if she is separated from you, say in somewhere like a museum. Such places will often have a tannoy system to call you.
- Agreeing that your child does not take side trips, even to see friends, without returning home first.
- Agreeing that a group of children stays together on trips to the park or swimming pool. They do not split up, even if they have an argument.
- An agreed time for your children to be home. This is easier if they have a watch and can tell the time.
- Helping them to practise their own address and telephone number until they can produce this confidently. This will be important if they do get lost, now or when they are older.
- Teach them to use a public telephone and provide them with coins or a phonecard as they get older. Explain how to make reverse charge calls.

Preparation and short trips

People have different opinions as to the right age for letting children go out on their own. Some children will nag you to let them do more than you are comfortable with, while others will cling and you may need to encourage them very firmly to branch out. Either way you can allow your child to do an increasing range of activities, either alone or accompanied by another child, so long as the trips are restricted to the hours of daylight. Part of letting go in this way has to involve teaching your child the rules of personal safety and ground rules for trips which we covered earlier. Depending on the area in which you live and the roads your children have to cross, you could introduce any of the activities given in the checklist below at some point during the five to eleven age range.

Loosening the reins – early activities

- Letting your child wander around a shop where you are also shopping.
- Letting her go into the shop next door to the one you are in.
- Allowing him to window shop in an arcade or small shopping centre a short distance from you.
- Cycling or roller skating round the block on the pavement.
- Walking to a nearby friend's house.
- Going to the local shop or video store. Initially you may like to chat with the owners or shop assistants to explain that you will let your child make the trip alone soon.
- Walking to and from school, if this is nearby. Perhaps cycling, later, if the roads are very quiet or your child can use cycle paths.
- Going to the local swimming pool or leisure centre with friends. (Many will not admit children under eight years unless accompanied by an adult.)
- Going to the park with friends.
- Walking to their nearby dance class or similar.
- Posting a letter for you.

Some parents are forced, for one reason or another, to allow children to make longer trips alone. Airlines have experience in looking after unaccompanied children, but do double-check the arrangements for meeting at the other end.

Learning to travel independently

Your child needs to learn how to travel about locally and eventually further afield. You may run him around in the car now but, even if you are willing, he will probably not want to be picked up by his parents when he's a teenager. Teach your children what they need to know while you are travelling with them. The guide below offers some practical suggestions.

Turning your child into a confident traveller

- Involve your five- and six-year-olds in recognising familiar routes and looking out for landmarks.
- As they get older and recognise routes, get your children to direct you home when you are walking or in the car.
- Involve your older children in planning routes – how you will get there by walking, car, bus or train.
- If you usually travel by car, do organise some trips using pubic transport in order to show your child:
  - how to read a bus or train timetable;
  - how to interpret a route guide, such as one of the London Underground;
  - how to plan a route with necessary changes;
  - what to do if you overshoot your bus stop or train station;
  - how to read a street map (this will be a mystery initially to your child since the 2-D page looks nothing like the 3-D landscape);
  - the beginnings of how to read a road map for the car, or a large-scale map for a walk;
  - how to pay for tickets on public transport, using machines for tickets, and how season tickets work;
  - how to go about asking for help if they get lost.

Speaking up for themselves

When your children were younger, you were their mouthpiece in communication with shopkeepers, nursery teachers, doctors, dentists and at the hospital. Increasingly now you won't be there to speak for them. Most of the time your child will have to speak up for herself at school. Some children become very anxious about exactly what they should say if they want to buy something in the local shop, or get a book out of the library. To help ease the process, encourage your child towards being the one to buy or to ask. She can practise with you what she will say if this is helpful to her. You then move steadily from saying it for her, to standing beside her as she speaks, to standing well away so that she is effectively doing it alone.

It is still appropriate that you should accompany your five to elevens to the doctor or dentist. However, do move towards encouraging your children to do the talking and to answer questions themselves. It may require a conscious effort for you to keep quiet. If necessary, politely ask the doctor or dentist to address questions to your child directly if this is not their style. You can, by all means, say your bit afterwards, but let your child speak first.

Some people can be remarkably rude to adults, let alone children, so you may need to be ready with an assertive approach on behalf of your child. This will help him to get satisfactory treatment now and will give him a model of acting assertively and not aggressively. (We suggested a couple of useful books for you earlier, on page 76.)

Final thoughts

You want children to become more and more able to move around safely and to know how to take care of themselves. It has to come – you may postpone it but you cannot avoid it. Teach them as well as you can and then let them go, little by little. Be pleased with what you and they are managing. Even if you are biting your nails for their safe return, your children will often come bouncing back home, full of excitement about how they bought the papers for you, or got out a video. Be excited with them. They will not realise how hard it was for you to let them go until they have children of their own.

CHAPTER EIGHT

Friends and friendship

Children aged between five and eleven are ever more aware of other children and adults around them. Friendships develop between children; some grow stronger, some fade away. Friends form groups that effectively exclude other children, although not necessarily unkindly. Increasingly, children become aware of what is expected of them, of the rules set by adults, and those set up by children themselves. In making friends, they will have to deal with the different outlooks of other families as expressed through their children.

Friendship

The path of friendship is not always smooth. There will be inevitable hitches. Best friends fall out over something that seems trivial to you, but is absolutely the final straw for them – at least for a few days; or your child's close friend moves away and he has trouble establishing another close friendship, since everybody else now seems to be taken. Boy–girl friendships get harder. Particularly with the over-eights, this sort of friendship can attract heavy teasing, with calls like 'he's your boyfriend' or 'you love her, yeech!' These are very normal problems which are virtually certain to occur at some time. Whilst parents can't prevent these, you can help by listening to your children when they are upset. You may be able to help them to establish better relationships with other children.

Making friends

The more contact your child has had with children of a similar age, the more likely it is that she will already have friends and has learned the skills of relating to other children. Being part of a group in school or in activities such as dance class or Brownies will help her to learn how to behave with other children. Sometimes, your children will need some discreet help from you.

Making contact

Your child may be in difficulties if he has had little contact with other children or is new to the district. You may need to help him by contacting other parents yourself or by arranging informal get-togethers between families, which may lead to opportunities to ask other children home to tea with yours. Similarly, you could take your child to a play or activity centre to provide the opportunity to meet children of a similar age. This does need to be done tactfully, however, because in the end it is up to your child who will be his friends.

Learning to relate to other children

If your child has been very isolated, for whatever reason, she may be baffled about how to talk and play with other children. You may gradually be able to improve this by creating opportunities for contact. If necessary chat with your child about possible topics of conversation with other children. Give him some hints about what kind of behaviour is likely to anger other children.

When your child stands out as different

Some quality in your child may make him genuinely different from local children of a similar age. Being different is not always a source of problems, but it can be.

If a child is very bright, this can sometimes mark him off from his easiest source of friends. Other children may reject him for being different, and may feel threatened. Your child may need the intellectual stimulation of an older group of children and of adults. However, he can still make friends with similar aged children through shared interests and activities.

If children are disabled, this can affect how friendships develop. If your child will attend a mainstream primary school, you may be able to help by discussing with the teacher, in advance, how you would like your child introduced, recognising her disability. Occasionally, children can be cruel to other children with disabilities, mainly through lack of understanding. With some honest information from adults, they may accept physical differences in a very straightforward manner; and many children can be very caring towards a friend who is unable to join in certain activities. Thereafter, the usual friendship rules apply. A six-year-old we know had a serious row with her friend, who was disabled. Her reason was that he had run her over twice, deliberately, with his wheelchair. Her anger was understandable and refreshingly without the pity that adults sometimes express.

Children learn adult prejudices

Your children may reject or be rejected by potential friends out of prejudice. One source of prejudice may be skin colour. Skin colour itself is not, of course, the problem; the problem comes with what people make of it. The same problems arise with prejudices based on sex or accent.

Children are alert and interested in differences between people. Even a baby of six months old is able to distinguish familiar from unfamiliar people. As a result, it is hardly surprising that many three-year-olds are perfectly able to notice differences in skin colour. Left to their own devices, children don't see this as anything other than just another difference between people. However, prejudiced attitudes are swiftly learned by young children who hear racist remarks from adults or other children. Cruel words based on racial prejudice are flung in all directions. White British children may insult black British children but the same children may unite together to be rude to children whose families originated in Asia or the Far East.

When children are fortunate enough to have the opportunity, many have friends of a different skin colour to themselves. If you make the effort to raise your children in a non-racist way, then they will look first for shared interests and happy companionship. Skin colour is not a good predictor of either of these. In any event, your children are bound to encounter racial prejudice sooner or later, so you need to be ready to talk about the issues honestly. If your children are more likely to be on the receiving end of racism, you will need to work hard to support them and to boost their confidence. You probably know this better than you would wish from your own personal experience.

It is perfectly reasonable for parents to expect teachers and school helpers to know how to step in effectively to support any child who is being insulted on the basis of what makes him or her an individual. This includes race and skin colour, sex and physical appearance. Some kinds of remarks should not go unchallenged.

Inviting friends round

Children have always enjoyed playing together. Previous generations went hurtling around the streets and parks, and while children of the 1990s still do this, many parents now tend to keep their children closer to home. There are a number of ways you can enable your children to spend time with their friends which do not leave you fretting for their safe return.

Different kinds of invitations

Depending on the space you have in your home, you may be able to offer:

- invitations to tea;
- invitations to join your family in an outing;
- stayovers – a friend sleeping at your house; and
- special teas and parties.

For any of these it is wise to sort out in advance whether your child's friend has any limitations as to what she or he eats. These may include likes and dislikes, allergies, or religious/family preferences for a particular diet.

Some children are ready for overnight stays sooner than others. Are you ready for it, both in terms of willingness and practical considerations? Have you an extra bed or space for a sleeping bag on the floor? Children often talk or play well into the late evening on sleepovers, so you may have some dozy children on your hands the following day.

Communicating your rules

It is worthwhile establishing a few key rules with your children, and with their friends.

Request advance warning of invitations   This applies equally for children coming to you or your child visiting elsewhere. It may not always be a lot of time, but it should certainly be more than a few minutes. This rule can be crucial with some children who are adept at such comments as, 'But I've asked Kelly to come this afternoon. You can't make me go back on that, I'll look stupid.'

When does tea become a party?   You can reasonably put a limit on how many friends your child has round at one time. Special teas and parties need more preparation, and will not be 'special' if they are too frequent. This is not just about food, either. Unless you have a good-sized garden and good weather, you will need to be present. More than three or four children of this age group need organising if your home is not to be a mess afterwards. It can be hard work.

Your house rules apply to everyone   Even basically well-behaved children can assume that something is okay to do in other people's homes if nobody has told them otherwise. Warn your children's friends if:

- some rooms in your home are off limits;
- some furniture is off limits, for example, filing cabinet, drawers, sewing basket;
- something looks like a plaything but absolutely is not, for example, your Japanese doll collection;
- items are off limits, for example, the computer or stereo, or there is a rule, like anyone banging the computer keys is removed immediately from the machine.

Don't make this a long list. Ensure that children register the really important things. It should help to avoid the disasters that make you most cross.

Disputes between friends

In the hurly-burly of playground life your children will have many disagreements and outright arguments. Close friends will occasionally fall out, and brothers and sisters will have the most ferocious fights in between happily getting on together. As a parent, you want to take your children's upset seriously whilst helping them be more able to tackle fraught situations in the future.

Other perspectives

It is hard for a five- or six-year-old to see an event through the eyes of someone else. In fights with other children, they will still tend to say 'Of course he meant to hurt me – he did hurt me!' Eight- and nine-year-olds may be more able to make a shrewd guess about intentions – 'She didn't see me, she didn't mean to bash into my arm.' They start to realise that their friends cannot read minds – 'He didn't know I hate wearing my glasses, usually I laugh at teasing.'

People come as a mixed package of the good and the not so good. Even your child's closest friend may do things that make her uncomfortable or irritated. For example, a very good friend may be incapable of knowing when to keep quiet; and your child will then learn, perhaps the hard way, not to share personal confidences with this particular friend, even though she may still be great company and offer support in the playground. Your child needs to tolerate other people's weaker points. Unrealistically high standards will lead to disappointment.

Children who are not sure of themselves sometimes feel better by putting others down. You can work with your child to try to prevent him taking insults to heart. But do, of course, show that you recognise that he has been hurt. Equally, lashing out at someone else may be temporary. Sometimes it happens in a particular situation, for example, children sometimes give their brothers or sisters a hard time when they have a friend round – it's a kind of showing off. Of course, having an understandable reason for doing something hurtful does not make it right. You would still want to tackle the child who showed off through belittling a brother or sister, otherwise putting someone else down may become a more lasting way for a child to behave. Bullying can then be a real problem. (We go into this in more detail later on, from page 111.)

Learning to negotiate

It would be unrealistic if you expected children never to squabble or fight. There will be arguments. Your objective is that your children learn possibilities other than slugging it out, physically or verbally, until everyone is hysterical. The great difficulty with fights is that each child wants to win. Fights make one person feel like the loser, which stokes up resentment – and a need to get even (revenge!) – for another time.

Your skill as a parent lies in deciding when and how to step in, because children will resolve some fights successfully themselves. However, you will need to intervene firmly from time to time and, by taking control, show children that you will not permit them to harm each other – either physically or emotionally. Sometimes you will be present at the scene; sometimes you will advise from a distance, in conversation with your child about what is happening at school.

The art of negotiation is to work towards a resolution that leaves the disputing children feeling that they have saved face, and that they have not been totally defeated. At root this requires all parties to focus on the issue, the problem to be resolved, rather than its effects or the personalities involved. You have to get the children away from the interminable 'Well he said, so I said . . .' If children can see benefits from the approach that you take, then they may well apply these themselves. Certainly, disputes in the home that are successfully resolved with your help will encourage your children to try similar tactics at school.

Dealing with disputes

In your own home, especially with your own children, you can work on all the following points. They also work just as well when you apply them to a group of children.

- Try to get them apart and to be quiet. They can be sullen, that's okay. Only raise your voice at first, if you are forced to get their attention, then continue at normal volume. It is often more effective to repeat what you are saying in exactly the same words and tone than to shout louder and louder.
- Ask *what* started this?, rather than *who* started this? This can make the fight less personal so that it can be looked at more dispassionately – not him, or her, but the events. Not who's right and who's wrong, but what happened? Get back to the initial problem.
- Look at ways to solve the problem. Is the argument about name calling, broken promises, violation of privacy? As shouting and

punching is not solving this, what other ways could be tried?

- Let everyone have their say without being shouted down. As an adult who is not taking sides, you should be able to get each child to listen a little to what the other one is saying.
- Advocate give and take. As chief negotiator and diplomat, your aim is to get both children to feel that in some sense they have won. Recognise that both children have a point, which removes the possibility of either party feeling that they have completely lost. Similarly, the total win can be removed. For example, as there was a noisy row, both winner and loser were at fault for getting out of control.
- Seek possible deals to help manage the conflict better in the future. For instance: a brother agrees to stop saying 'you're just a girl' and the sister agrees to stop calling him a 'fathead' – the critical words you have identified from your children's arguments; or no one takes any books from someone else's bedroom without asking first – this is basic courtesy; or your child lets his friend borrow his bike, and in return he lets your child borrow his skateboard – a temporary swap.
- Encourage your children to walk away from a fist fight in the home. Let it be known that once the hitting starts, the children involved will be separated and you will not be at all interested in who started it – but that *you* will finish it. Work to establish that in your house you are more supportive when children walk away and tell an adult that there is a dispute, than when they start to punch or kick. Be prepared to explain the difference, as you see it, between appropriate telling and 'tale-telling'.

You need to focus on whatever the problem is and get the personalities away from centre stage. Your children need to recognise that they would both benefit if the problem was satisfactorily and permanently resolved. If they have absolutely no concern for the other person involved, or their views, then on the one hand fights are more likely, and on the other, and this is the powerful argument, why on earth bother to fight?

Emotional wear and tear on you

Dealing with squabbling children is very wearing indeed. You may be clear on the calm and reasoned approach you want to take, but there will be times when your children explode into conflict when you are exhausted or are totally absorbed in something important like driving through heavy traffic. Under these circumstances, you may do no more than yell at them to 'Shut up!' Your children will survive this, especially if you usually manage to remain calm. They will realise that they have driven you to the very edge. Talk to them as soon as things are calmer and try to sort out what remains of their argument (if they haven't already forgotten it).

Hollering at your children on a regular basis is not advisable, if for no other reason than that they will give up listening to you altogether. It is also, of course, ludicrous to be telling your children to stop shouting if you don't make any effort to stop doing this yourself.

There is no magical way of saving yourself from feeling worn out and aggravated, but there are several things which may help.

Spend time with other adults   Firstly, you do need some adult conversation sometimes. Chatting with five to elevens becomes increasingly interesting, since their topics of conversation get broader. However, they would probably be the first to say that they like to talk with people of their own age as well as with you. So there is no shame in your wanting some adult company.

If you have a partner, do you create time just to be together and chat — not always about the children? Can you make time to talk with other adults who are not family? If you work outside your home, some of your needs for adult company may be met, but at the cost of other sources of wear and tear.

Share experiences with fellow parents   It is very possible to chat with other parents generally about children without grousing in a disloyal way about your own. You will find out that some of what you're facing is not unusual and you may get some good ideas.

You may also find out that your child's complaints about school dinners or a child who bullies are not isolated gripes. You may usefully get together with other parents to tackle the problem.

Time to yourself for what you want to do   You may greet this suggestion with a hollow laugh. Nevertheless, do look carefully at whether you can find some part of your week in which you could do what you would like. Useful slots of time for you may be very short. For example, if you have just split up your warring children, you may find that sitting and having a cup of coffee calms you down.

Start again with a clean slate   Once you've dealt with an incident, let it go. Don't keep chewing it over in your mind. If you feel you have to, then tell your partner or a friend (not in front of the children) and then let it go.

Pressures from friends

Children will experience strong pressure from their friends to adopt the group line on behaviour or habits. Some of this may be harmless imitation, although it may endanger you financially. We covered some of the pressures regarding possessions and fashionable clothes in Chapter 6; but on other occasions, the pressure may threaten your child's health and well being.

Risky activities

Problems often arise from the pressures exerted by friends or even acquaintances to conform to what is supposed to be exciting or grown-up. Your child understandably wants to be accepted, and it takes strength to stand out alone. An answer of 'It's not good for me' or 'I'm not supposed to' sounds weak to children and is likely to be met with hoots of derision.

Nobody has come up with a guaranteed way of protecting your children. However, the more successful health education programmes have tackled directly what children and young teenagers will say and do in response to pressure from friends. Through talking with your children you may be able, together, to anticipate some of the pressures they could face. You will help your children by doing the following:

Spend time with your children

- Be as generous with your time as you can manage. Make sure that your children have plenty of inexpensive fun as well as the treats which drain your money. Chapter 9 covers activities you can do together.
- Encourage your children in a range of interests. Help them to learn to occupy themselves safely and happily. Some children who drift into smoking or glue sniffing are very, very bored.

Keep talking with your children

- Reassure them over the years that they can come to you with problems. Even though you cannot promise not to worry or never to get cross, you can and must promise to stand by them and help them resolve problems. Sometimes this will involve them accepting the consequences of their actions.
- In a number of conversations, talk over with your children the whole business of being pressured to do something you know you really should not. This is likely to come up in other contexts, for example, foolish dares from which your child does not know how to escape or pressure to join in the bullying of another child.
- Coach your child in the possible escape strategies. These can include teaching your child assertiveness – the basic right to say 'No' without explanation or justification. Your child has the right to say firmly, 'No, I don't want to.' This applies as much to calls to join in bullying as to join the smokers behind the shed. Also, talking over how your child might stress the health aspects in their 'No' but express this assertively. They

might feel comfortable saying things like, 'You want to end up dead, you go ahead. I'm not that stupid.' or 'I don't care to smell like an old ashtray.' Talk over what your children could say to help them feel strong. They can practise phrases with you, if they want.

At some point your children will face the pressure of 'this is the grown-up thing to do.' Teach them to take an assertive hold on the exchange. Perhaps they could say something like, 'I can't believe it, you really think this stuff is grown-up. I've got better things to do with my time!' Get across to your children that they don't have to apologise or defend their decision to walk away from an activity that they know is dangerous or cruel to someone else. It is their right to walk away. However, your children will not always manage to extricate themselves, so they must feel confident that they can come to you and you will help and support them.

Keep watching your children

If they start to show any of the tell-tale health signs of the hazardous activities, tackle this with them sooner rather than later. Smoking, solvent abuse and drinking alcohol will probably leave a smell about your children or on their clothes. Their general health will probably be affected by this, or by the use of drugs. Their behaviour or moods may change. We go into more detail about this in Chapter 7.

Bullying

Children have always been a source of occasional trouble to each other. There is no absolute time when teasing and wind-ups become unpleasant. Some children can shrug off unfriendly behaviour that is a torment to others. There is no doubt, however, that bullying is a fact of life for children, either because they are on the receiving end or they know a child who is being bullied.

What is bullying?

Bullying is one kind of aggressive behaviour. It is intended to hurt – physically, emotionally, or both. Bullying may be carried out by one child alone, or sometimes in an organised group. The child, or children, doing the bullying are seen as stronger than the victim, and this need not necessarily mean physically bigger or stronger. Bullies are likely to be either the same age as their victims or older. They may be of either sex.

Bullying is unprovoked in the sense that the victim has not done anything that would normally be seen as deserving retaliation. It is a repeated pattern of behaviour, not an isolated incident caused by temper or frustration. Victims of bullying can be driven to such despair, because there seems to be no escape. Even if they tell adults, their unhappiness is not always taken seriously.

The bully characteristically picks on something different about the other child. This may be height, skin colour, wearing glasses or being overweight. Children have been bullied on class grounds – for being working class or for being 'posh'.

People often think of bullying as being largely physical – as attacks ranging from regular kicks and shoves to an organised beating up. Some bullying is of this kind, while some has a sexual connotation where boys chase girls in order to look up their skirts or force kisses on them. It can also take the form of threats, say, of being beaten up if the victim doesn't hand over money or possessions.

However, another type of bullying involves long-term teasing and jibes – which can seriously distress some children. The child who is bullying may fall back on the claim 'It's just a joke', but this is obviously not true, since the bully shows no intention of stopping even when the victim is obviously upset. A joke is something that is enjoyed by both parties.

Why do some children bully?

There is no single reason why some children learn to bully, but there are a number of different possibilities:

- They may have found no other way to deal with their own stress and upset. They may feel incompetent in their school work; or younger children may be upset by the arrival of a new baby. (Not all children cope with stress by bullying other children, of course.)
- They may feel stronger, more in control by bullying, and the feeling of power becomes addictive. They may find it hard to express themselves, and therefore resort to name calling or physical means to win arguments.
- Some children who have been spoiled rotten expect everyone to do what they want and resort to bullying when other children won't cooperate.
- Some children who have been hurt or abused in some way find this a means of getting back at the world in general. Or if children themselves have been bullied, then they may later take revenge – by bullying others.
- A child may have fallen in with a crowd who bully. If he doesn't join in, he has no friends.

Helping your child

Your child may tell you that he or she is having serious trouble with another child. Alternatively, children do not say anything, because they do not believe that anybody can help them. It may be that they feel a failure because they are a victim. Whatever the reason, it is very important that you watch out for changes in your children's behaviour which could signal that they are being bullied – physically or by cruel words.

Signs that a child is being bullied

Watch out for changes in your child's behaviour such as:

- Not wanting to go to school, or wanting you to take her to school when she has been happy to go alone.
- Unexplained bruises and torn clothes beyond what has been normal for your child up to now.
- Pocket money, dinner money or possessions regularly going missing.
- Getting upset very easily, crying, withdrawing into himself, stammering.
- A pattern of nightmares.
- Beginning to do poorly in her school work.
- Trying to harm herself or talking as if life is no longer worth living. (A few children, bullied beyond endurance, have attempted suicide, sometimes successfully.)

There is no way you can ensure that your child is never bullied, but you may be able to prevent a situation going from bad to worse. Often children are given the advice 'Ignore it, it'll stop in the end.' Indeed it will, but if the bullying is serious, the end may be months or even years away, by which time your child could be seriously damaged emotionally, if not physically. In contrast, some parents go to the other extreme and tell their children, especially their boys, to hit back at every opportunity. Although we, ourselves, do not support the opposite stance of 'never, ever hit back', our strong recommendation is that parents position this as a last resort.

Ignoring and avoiding

There is ignoring and there is retreat. The kind of behaviour that may help your child is to learn to turn away from a child who is being insulting, in such a way that it does not look like a retreat or defeat. Your child may feel able to practise with you:

- a contemptuous shrug of the shoulders;
- a withering sneer; or
- looking someone straight in the eye, along with saying 'No!' or 'You can pack that in right now!'

Children should not have to change all their normal habits in order to avoid a child or a group who bullies. In theory, it shouldn't be your child's responsibility to keep away, but it may help as a temporary measure. With no victim to taunt for a while the bully may move on. For example, if the problem happens on the way home, some changes of route may help. Ultimately, it is the responsibility of the child who is doing the bullying to behave in an acceptable way. It is the responsibility of adults – parents, teachers, playground supervisors – to make sure bullying, and any opportunities for it, are removed as far as possible. If playground problems are focused on vital areas like the toilets, the headteacher and all the staff should be doing something about the problem. The consequences of bullying should not be rewarding to the bully.

Self-defence

The skills of self-defence in dealing with bullying are both physical and psychological.

Get together with friends   Alert your child to the strategy of strength in numbers. Some children who bully are looking for the child who seems to have no support.

Verbal self-defence   Although words may not deter the very physical bully they will often work otherwise. Being good with words can help the child on the receiving end to feel stronger. Don't put your child in a weaker position by insisting that she must always be nice to people – bullies don't deserve it. Give your child permission to shout at another child who is bullying him. Allow children to practise yelling 'No!' or 'Shove off!' and then stalking angrily away if it helps.

Help your child to practise an assertive reply, and not to accept the grounds laid out by the bully. Your child should not defend herself by saying 'I'm not a swot' or 'It's not my fault I'm short.' Teach your child to take the high road of 'Sure I limp, what's it to you?', 'You have a problem with that?' or 'Of course I'm black and I'm proud of it.' Your child is accepting what the bully says as self-evidently true but she is turning it into the bully's problem or something that is a source of pride. It is very difficult to get any pleasure out of goading someone who refuses to be upset.

Help your child to have some sharp ripostes ready. These can include replies for anything that your child feels makes her more vulnerable to insults.

Physical defence   This includes body language, so help your child to practise walking tall. He needs to stand straight and not slouch, looking as if he expects someone to hit him over the head. Children are less likely to pick on other children who look confident and decided.

Your child could also learn physical self-defence. This could be in the form of classes, or simple lessons you give yourself. The very fact that children feel confident that they could defend themselves physically can give out a message, through body language, that dissuades the bullies.

Schools often ask parents to tell their children not to hit back, on the grounds that it only makes things worse. This is a reasonable request *only* if the school, with all the staff, is dealing effectively with those pupils who start the hitting, shoving and punching. Otherwise the better behaved children are being required to solve the problem through their tolerance of being mistreated. Some schools fail to come to terms with the reality that a proportion of their pupils believe that beating up and verbally threatening other children is a sign of power and prestige. If school policy and practice is not effectively kerbing these children, you may come to the decision, as a parent, that you will give your children permission to defend themselves physically if need be. If you decide to do this, then:

- ensure that your children understand that this occurs only in response to persistent aggression, not to initiate fights;
- carefully talk through with your child the kind of circumstances that you feel could justify a physical response;
- go through all the other strategies, including telling a teacher or playground helper as well;
- stress that physical retaliation must be your child's last resort;
- make it clear to your child that this is not a strategy you will tolerate in your home; and
- be prepared to stand by your children if they get into trouble for defending themselves physically.

Tackling the school

If your child is being bullied within school grounds or by fellow pupils on the journeys to or from school, then you need to contact the school. Look back to Chapter 3 for more general suggestions about developing a positive working relationship with your child's school. You may have to point out that your child has tried to tell a teacher or playground supervisor what is happening and nothing has been done to help. You might explain that you have found out the reason for your child's unhappiness or his many bruises. In more general terms, you may press for a school policy on handling bullying or a strategy to handle a particularly troublesome kind of bullying. Parents have a right to expect schools to have a clear policy on rules for children's behaviour and strategies for violations of these rules. Dealing firmly with bullying is part of this.

If your child is the bully

Somebody's children are doing the bullying. To your horror, you may find out that it's your son or daughter. You may get this message directly from your child's teacher or from other children. A more roundabout warning can be that the children you would like to be friendly with your son or daughter seem unwilling to accept your child's invitations. (Don't forget, that there are, of course, any number of reasons besides bullying that lead children to refuse an invitation.) However you find out, you may not want to believe it. But, in order to help your child you need to check it out. You can talk with your child, although you may not get a straight answer. Alternatively, you can brace yourself to talk with other parents who may tell you the truth, if you don't immediately get angry with them.

What can you do?

You need to remain as calm as possible, don't pitch into your child, don't bully him. Make it clear to your child that whilst you will stand by her as a parent, you will not support this kind of behaviour. Set out realistic and firm boundaries to what you believe is acceptable behaviour towards other children. Talk through with your child what appears to have started the bullying behaviour. Look back at the earlier list of the different reasons why children bully. For example, can you help your child to find other ways to feel confident?

Seriously consider getting your child to apologise to any child he has hurt – physically or emotionally. This may be in person, or it could be a letter. Consider also getting your child to give back, or pay back, anything taken from another child. This needs careful handling, since your child will be resentful if he loses face entirely. If the whole situation looks very complicated and is muddled up with serious stress in the family, you should consider some help for all of you. The local Child Guidance Centre may make a suggestion for family counselling.

For your information

The organisation, *Kidscape*, has practical material on bullying and about developing a school policy on this problem. Contact them at: World Trade Centre, Europe House, London E1 9AA. Tel: 071-488-2400.

Final thoughts

As social animals, your children need friends. They need other children to play with and to share interests, and most of the time this will go smoothly. Your children need to be confident that they can turn to you for support when they want it and be fairly sure that your way of helping will not embarrass them.

They can enjoy being with you, yet you cannot substitute for other children. In the company of friends, they can indulge in the kind of playground gossip that they judge will not interest you. They can talk at length on topics that do not hold your attention, such as endless discussion of the merits of different video games or television programmes. They also need other children for the times that they want to complain about adults – you or their teachers – or to talk about things that they judge are not fit for your ears.

CHAPTER NINE

Doing things together

Spending time with your children is your major gift to them. This may be hard to organise, particularly at stressful times in your life, but it will be appreciated more in the end than buying them things instead of giving them time.

Physical activities and games

Not all children will be champion athletes or successful footballers, but if your child does develop a talent, then you will naturally want to nurture this. However, encouraging your children in physical activity and joining in with them is important for many other reasons.

Playing games with children is usually enjoyable, although not without its moments. Children, like adults, may take games very seriously. We have spent some supposedly casual football games involving eight- to ten-year-olds with several team members sitting in a tree as a protest at the referee's decision. More importantly, everyone needs to use their body as well as their brain. Although exercise can be overdone, most surveys suggest that nowadays many adults, along with their children, do less physical activity than is ideal for their health.

You can encourage your children to try out different activities and to feel competent in their own chosen areas. Everything that we said about learning in Chapter 2 holds good here – encouragement, the need to practise and to boost your child's confidence through the difficult stages and after something has gone wrong.

Your child may have a specific reason for being either under- or over-confident, from previous experience or from their physical condition. Children who have taken a bad fall or who have been made to look foolish may be very resistant to try again. Some children recover their confidence, but others shift their worry from a specific incident ('I hurt my knee climbing') to the general ('I'll hurt myself if I do any physical activity').

Finding somewhere to play

Not everyone is lucky enough to have a big garden to absorb the range of physical games that children want and need to play. Some things you may not mind them doing inside – somersaults on the carpet are not usually troublesome unless children crash into something, and headstands against the wall may be restricted to a room where you don't care about the wallpaper. However, bikes, roller skates and football games are outdoor activities in adult minds, if not in children's.

If your children are nearer to five than eleven, they will need supervision outside the house. They also need to be taught safe behaviour near roads, and consideration for other people and their property. As children get older you relax your level of supervision, although it can be hard, and let them cycle outside alone and go to play in parks with other children. (We cover this in Chapter 7.) If you don't have a play area nearby or you don't trust your neighbourhood, then you will need to be prepared to organise outings with your five to elevens, or they will be bouncing off the walls of your home. Some towns and cities have flexible school holiday programmes for little or no cost. Also, there are often play camps for the over-fives, for which you pay, sometimes rather heavily.

Physical activities with your children

Children in middle childhood tend to be pleased if you play with them. It is more likely to be your teenagers who make cutting remarks about your level of skill, or who have very stereotyped notions about how parents should behave. The opportunities for organised physical activities and classes may be greater if you live in a town or city. If you live away from large towns, you may have to draw mainly on your own resources or get organised with some other families whose children have similar interests. Sharing the travel arrangements to get a group of children to a club or class may be the answer.

Do think broadly about what your child could do, both alone and with your involvement. The activities below offer a range of ideas, perhaps with more possibilities than you remember from your own childhood. Choose what *you* could enjoy doing, as well as your child.

- The park or open space for any of the following:
  - football, in which Mums can play as well as Dads;
  - throwing and catching balls or frisbees;
  - flying kites or model airplanes;
  - cricket, rounders, or baseball;
  - climbing;
  - tennis;
  - using the play park equipment (you may still need to push your child on the swings for the early part of this age group);
  - roller-skating or skateboarding – Perhaps have a go yourself, but do remember that you will fall more heavily than your child!
- An adventure playground which gives children the opportunity to enjoy the broader kinds of physical activity that these offer.

DOING THINGS TOGETHER

Most do not allow adults in unless their children are under five, so you will not be able to enjoy yourself on the poles and catwalks.

- Swimming – Many five to elevens learn to swim, often helped through school lessons as well as by you. Once your children are competent, you may get the chance to swim, after years of standing about, being splashed and resisting entreaties from children to throw them.

- Revive an old hobby with your children, or involve your children in an existing activity now they are older. For example, Jennie had a wonderful excuse to return to ice-skating – abandoned since her teenage years – when our daughter became interested after watching the championships on television. Similarly our son became interested in tennis after watching Wimbledon.

- If you do a regular programme of exercise, your children may join in. Some have specific exercises for children as young as six. If you are in any doubt, take advice, since some kinds of highly vigorous exercise are unsuitable for children.

- Gardening can include weeding, raking up grass cuttings or leaves and, most popular in our household, pruning. Teach your children proper use of gardening tools and the importance of hand washing after contact with earth and plants.

- Cycling also provides a good opportunity to tackle road drill. (See Chapter 7 on road safety.)

- Hiking can be enjoyable for children, particularly if you have discovered what excites them, like water or woods. Hikes should not be too demanding and you may need to walk yourself in as well as your children. Eventually, nine- and ten-year-olds can walk distances of about eight to ten miles over a day, so long as there are breaks for picnics or pub lunches. Walking can be a good opportunity for chatting. It's also an opportunity to interest your child in a whole range of subjects, from bird watching to geology, from trees and flowers to history.

- Sports centres and leisure centres now offer an increasing range of facilities. You may be able to arrange a game of squash for when your daughter attends her trampolining class. You might all enjoy short tennis.

Building up

Look at the possibilities and if your main exercise has become operating the remote control on the television, consider taking a step-by-step approach to incorporate more physical activity into your lives together. You can build up steadily. Get the children used to walking, for instance, through round-the-block walks on warm summer evenings. Short games are better initially, both because children's interest span at this age can be short, and to ensure that no one ends up totally exhausted.

Consider using incentives at this training stage, so long as they don't dominate the whole activity. You might promise an ice-cream on the way home, provided you don't have to carry your child or all their gear.

Keep it fun

You may want your children to persevere with an activity that they take up and not flit from one thing to another – particularly if it's a course of lessons. You do need, however, to keep an eye out that what is supposed to be enjoyable isn't becoming a form of drudgery for your child.

Some children will take on lots of late afternoon or weekend activities with great enthusiasm. If they look exhausted or resist getting ready for one of their many clubs, you may want, with their agreement, to prune their social calendar. Similarly, you may wish to set limits to protect your own sanity. It may feel as if you have the role of full-time chauffeur for activities that you cannot join.

Sit-down games

Children can get very bored and this isn't solved by buying them even more toys. It's not always possible to go out to share some of the physical activities suggested earlier, and children will probably watch too much television or play non-stop computer games, unless you offer them alternatives. Certainly, if you want to place a time limit on these activities, this is sensible, but you do need to be available to respond to the cry of 'What can I do?'

Shared time with your children can be special but does not have to mean expensive treats or unrelenting excitement. The joy of the over-fives is that they become more and more able to enjoy a sit-down activity that can hold your attention as well. Consider some of the following:

- Jigsaws – Children may enjoy doing the simpler ones on their own. The more challenging ones can be tackled as a family. Spread them out on a table or large tray, so you don't try to complete a huge jigsaw all in one sitting.
- Card games – Five- and six-year-olds will still enjoy games like Happy Families, but very soon they will be ready to use a conventional pack of cards. Start them off with simple games like Snap, Beat your neighbour out of doors and Cheat. Then introduce the games that will help them to understand about suits, how to win cards and the idea of trumping. Teach them games like Knock out whist, German whist and, later, Solo. It's possible to teach children a simplified version of a game like Cribbage and then to teach the full game when they are confident. Some children really like playing Patience and there are many different versions.
- Board games and games with pieces – Your children will be ready to move from picture dominoes to ones with numbers. They may enjoy tiddly winks. They will also be ready for board games. From the ever-increasing range, pick the ones you can

all enjoy. Snakes and ladders or any simple 'moving round the squares' game will start you off. Adults and older children have to be patient with the younger ones. You all have to cope with the potential problem of winners and losers.

Games like Scrabble and Monopoly are also sneaky ways of giving your children practice in the skills of spelling and adding up. Consider teaching your eight- or nine-year-olds draughts, backgammon and then chess. Initially you may need to give yourself a handicap to even up the odds of victory. Once they have learned the rules, children will be happy to play card and board games with each other, or alone.

If you travel distances with your children or take holidays away from home, it's worth investing in a travelling games set as well as the larger home versions.

- Television and videos – As your children get older, it's easier to find programmes and videos that are both suitable for them and might also interest you. Take a careful look at the week's or day's programmes with your children and encourage them to make an active choice, rather than switching without thought between channels. Look out for programmes on subjects that may interest your children. Some televised adaptations may hold your children's interest, whilst the original book or play might be too hard for them at the moment. Some of the adult evening programmes on nature, science topics or history can be equally interesting to children. Consider videoing either the whole programme or the relevant part. Watch it together.
- Music – You can listen to each other's music. It's not inevitable that they will hate your choice and vice versa. Since a certain amount of popular music gets recycled, you may find that you own the original of a recently released single.

For your information

Try *The complete Hoyle's games*, brought up to date by Lawrence H. Dawson (Routledge and Kegan Paul, 1989).

This book covers the rules for a wide range of card and board games, as well as games like darts and snooker. Also, for a good source of indoor and outdoor games, try: *Children's games* by Gyles Brandreth (Chancellor Press, 1992).

Hobbies and interests

Hobbies will stand your child in good stead for the future. It's handy for them to learn that doing something satisfying doesn't always have to cost money or involve expensive technology. Hobbies can also help children to concentrate and persist in seeing a project through to completion.

Hobbies are also a chance to show that just because someone isn't talented in one area, say painting, doesn't mean that he or she has no creativity. It can be applied elsewhere in model-making or creative writing. Your children are likely to be offered a range of activities at school. However, there is every reason to equip yourself at home for those they enjoy the most, or for some new ones.

Joining in and getting started

Your company is likely to be an added bonus. Your children are more likely to persevere with your help and largely undivided attention, and you will manage this more easily if you are motivated. So, as well as seeing what interests your child, ask yourself, 'What would I enjoy doing?' Watch out, however, that you don't end up in direct competition with your son or daughter, with the possibility that you may produce more impressive work than them.

There are many good craft books available, and initially the most useful are those which introduce a number of crafts at the basic level of skill. Sometimes magazines will have a good illustrated introduction to a craft. Television can also be an inspiration, so long as you and your child don't get discouraged if your effort fails to reach the standard of the 'one they made earlier' on the programme. Where possible, find materials within your home, buy-

ing just a few basics. There are many ready-boxed starter kits available for crafts, but this is usually a relatively expensive way of
equipping yourself.

It is important to give your sons and daughters access to a range
of activities. There is no more reason to stop boys knitting and girls
doing woodwork than there would be to discourage the reverse on
the grounds that it is too traditional.

Drawing and painting

Clearly, painting is not the cleanest of activities, but it is worth
finding somewhere for them to try, where the inevitable spilt water
pot will cause least damage. Your children will need a store of
brushes, pencils, pens and crayons, or perhaps chalks. If you hid
the felt-tips in desperation when your children were younger, you
could consider bringing them out again now. Keep costs down by
using any sources of scrap paper that you can. Do find somewhere
to display your children's artwork – on a board or with magnetic
holders on the fridge.

Collections

Your child may be most interested in collecting round a theme.
Hobbies like stamp collecting may involve more expense, but do
not have to get out of control. Scrapbook collections can cost next
to nothing and can be built from tickets, tin labels, postcards or
pressed flowers.

Crafts

Children can learn to knit but this is a difficult skill to manage. It
involves a number of coordinated actions that have to work
together. Encouragement and patience are required. Try them with
patterns where the final size and shape is not too crucial.

If they are interested in needlework, large hole tapestry work
with a blunt tapestry needle is a good way to start. This kind of

canvas is called binca. Children who are interested can progress to more intricate work and to sewing material together to make something. Do be ready to unravel sewing tangles for your children. Some under-elevens may learn to handle a sewing machine. An old fashioned hand machine, if you have got one, may be easier to control for the beginner.

Simple weaving can be an absorbing hobby for children. It's easier with a small weaving loom but still possible and cheaper to weave on card scored with slats to take the wool.

Beadwork uses similar skills to needlework. Some impressive items can be made from simple threading. If your ten- or eleven-year-old enjoys this, she or he may be ready for a beading loom. Modelling clay can also be used to make beads to thread.

Paper work is fiddly and needs patience, but can yield good end results. These can be three-dimensional models using paper and card, and usually unbelievable amounts of Sellotape and glue. Some craft books have excellent ideas for simple paper engineering and give instructions for very effective pop-up cards which children can manage. Tissue flowers can work well too. The Japanese craft of origami offers both simple and complicated models.

Macramé is a craft that seems to have gone out of fashion since the 1970s. However, if you can find a shop that sells the jute and T-pins for holding the work, your children might well take to macramé. It is possible to make impressive small and large items quite rapidly once the basic knotting techniques have been grasped.

Modelling

This can be with bought or home-made play dough. Children can progress to using clay that dries without putting it in an oven or the more expensive coloured clays that can be baked in an ordinary oven and then varnished. Collage and junk modelling can be virtually free – try egg boxes, small bits of material or wool, silver paper wrappings, pasta, flowers and leaves.

Some seven- or eight-year-olds will be interested in plastic model kits. Wood, card and plastic kits are also available to build land-scapes and towns. Balsa wood kits are possible, but require the use of extremely sharp knives, which will mean you will need to supervise closely.

Woodwork

This also needs close supervision, preferably by an adult with basic skills in making the tools do what they are supposed to. As with modelling kits, you will need some non-negotiable rules about where woodworking is done. It will be too late when your son or daughter's great work is nailed to your best polished table.

Printing and dyeing

For simple printing you can use a thick mix of powder paint and everyday objects like chunks of fruit or cotton reels. Print onto paper or fabric. As with painting, you need to cover your child in a large apron and work on a wipeable plastic cloth. If you can't easily wipe the floor, then put down newspaper. Simple tie-dyeing works well using string, clothes pegs, corks or elastic bands to tie up old tee-shirts or just pieces of light coloured cloth. The dyes from a haberdashery counter work well.

Music

Most children learn to enjoy listening to and making some kind of music, although only some are motivated to learn to play an instrument more challenging than a triangle or a kazoo. If your child is interested, do try to give them a go. You can sometimes buy second-hand instruments but a cheaper alternative is to try to borrow one until it's clear whether your child is going to continue. Your child will need to be willing to practise on a regular basis. Try to agree on a schedule which doesn't ruin leisure times for either of you. Initially, practice times can be hard on everyone, depending on the loudness of the instrument and how soon your child learns to hold a tune.

Working with your children

In any of the suggested activities, your children may need help through the stage where nothing seems to come out to their satisfaction. Help them to finish something, if necessary, and to have it put in pride of place.

Children sometimes fail to see how their efforts have improved and they need to be distracted from concentrating miserably on how, say, in contrast to their own creations, their elder brother's Lego models never fall apart.

Use of tools

Teaching children to use tools properly and safely progresses through the same stages as learning how to work independently given in Chapter 5. You go from 'Let me do that for you' through 'You do it but let me help' to 'You try it now on your own'. All of these steps need to be completed before you are happy to say, 'Yes, you can borrow my hammer, but I want it back.' Of course, unsupervised children could damage themselves, or your home, doing a number of crafts, but only if they are left alone before they can use the necessary tools safely. You can teach your children bit by bit to handle tools that will do the job. You make your own decision when, for example, you'll allow scissors that really cut or access to a proper chisel.

Between the ages of five and eleven, children develop a growing sense of pride and appreciate more and more how professional their work can be. This often stems from a growing competence in using the real tools designed to the job rather than the child's equivalent.

Clearing up

Increasingly, children should be helping you to clear up, if not actually doing it themselves. All the hobbies we have mentioned leave some debris – in some cases a considerable amount! Cleaning equipment and putting it away may be boring, but this is not a good reason why parents should be left to do it. Children may find it more tolerable if you clear up with them, chatting together.

Final thoughts

Your children will vary in their skills in different areas. Some will have a very good sense of balance, whilst others will pick up coordination skills, like skipping, faster. Some children will have great difficulty in fine handicrafts, yet produce dramatic, sweeping paintings.

More energetic physical skills will help keep children healthy. They can be good fun and may well encourage them to work alongside other children. However, team games will not necessarily build either cooperation or dispassionate losing. Whatever adults say about the point of games, children will swiftly understand if the real objective is to win – they are not stupid.

Your involvement with your children's hobbies can help their concentration, particularly during the bad times when it all seems to go wrong. It can work, at least partly, against any restriction from the stereotypes held by others. There are still plenty of people who claim, 'She's a girl, she won't be any good at woodwork' or 'He's a boy, he'll be all fingers and thumbs at knitting.' Most importantly, enjoy yourself in these activities – they can be fun, despite the glue on your clothes and bits of paper all over the kitchen table. You can learn something too. Perhaps you may recapture that feeling, from the years before you had children, when there was time to do something just because you felt like doing it.

Conclusions: Growing together

The knowledge and skills required to be a good parent are extraordinarily wide-ranging. If you listed all the different tasks that you take on as a parent and then converted them into jobs that other people do for money, you would probably have at least a dozen. Added to this, you are expected to deliver the practical skills of negotiation, counselling and plea bargaining – all with the flair of someone skilled in time management. Do remember that this all adds up to a tough assignment for anyone.

Lots of parents do very well by their families. Part of the survival trick is to focus as much on what you are good at as on those skills or problems that are causing you some trouble at the moment. Forget perfect parenting, you will wear yourself out. The best parents are those who are willing to start each day afresh and to forgive their children's horrible moments – just as you hope that they will forgive you yours. You don't know it all and there is no need to pretend that you do.

Do remember to look after yourself; not just because your children need you to be fit and healthy, but for your own sake. Make sure that you eat properly and get your rest, as well as checking up on your children's welfare. You are allowed to put your feet up sometimes, and to do something just because you would enjoy doing it.

As parents, you are working models of how to run an adult life. Your children will watch and copy you. You don't have to pretend that you never have difficulty making decisions or that you never make mistakes. Your children can learn from seeing how you try to weigh up all the issues as you come to a difficult crossroads. If they never see you make a mistake, then your children can't learn from you how they might be able to put something right, or sometimes just have to live with it. In so many things, you can teach your child in ways that school never can.

If you are a two-parent family, it isn't compulsory that mothers and fathers try to be identical kinds of parent. You may not be able to do this anyway. Fathers are still more likely than mothers to work without interruption, unless they are hit by redundancy. Mothers take time off to have children, although for some women this is only a very short period of time.

Holding down a job will reduce the time any parent can spend with the family. This is true whether you are a woman or a man, and is a difficult problem to resolve. You need to secure your job and your family's income, yet you want to spend time with your family. You will need to be prepared to think over your priorities. Make sure that your paid work isn't eating more into family time than is strictly necessary. If you are very ambitious in your career, don't expect your children, or your partner, to wait interminably for you to pay them some attention. When you have a family, you have to make choices. Regardless of what some people will claim, it isn't possible to have it all.

As parents you will have to decide between yourselves who does what in the family. Your children will build a picture of what is 'normal' in adult life from their experiences in their own home. Make sure you put your principles into practice – children will soon find you out if you are big on talk about equality between the sexes and yet expect a daughter to help around the house more than a

CONCLUSIONS: GROWING TOGETHER

son. You will also have to resolve any serious differences of opinion over child rearing between parents or other family members. You may find, as your children get older, that you especially disagree on the age at which children should be given freedom to do things on their own. Don't argue these out in front of the children. Sometimes it will be possible to allow your children to make their own choices, so long as this doesn't compromise their safety.

You have every right to your own beliefs about how people should behave and to your own religious or philosophical outlook on life. You owe it to your children to explain what you believe and your reasons, but try not to impose your views on them. They may, in the end, share your opinions, but insisting that they fall into line now will not make that more likely.

Between the ages of five and eleven, children will spend more time under the influence of adults and children outside the family. They do things without you, and demand to do more. They have learned so much and yet, as you know, they still have a great deal to understand. Parents have to learn to let go, however difficult this may be. Children must have the opportunity to experiment and try things for themselves. Each family – and each member – will need to work out their own feelings and approach, recognising that without independence there is no growing up.

Throughout these years with your children you will need huge reserves of patience if you are to help them. Great persistence is also required to get messages across and to build your child's approach to life. (If only one could depend on saying it just the once!) Do remember that children are not spoiled by attention as such, only by too much of the wrong sort of attention, or by material goodies instead of adult time. Children need attention that focuses sometimes on their wants and needs. They deserve the security of a sense of belonging and of being accepted for themselves.

Keep to a habit of watching your children as well as listening to them, since they will not tell you everything, nor will they always have the words to explain their increasingly complex view of the world. Without good information, your position as a parent is founded in quicksand.

You cannot protect your children against life or make everything all right for them. This is impossible, so don't even try. You can help them learn ways of coping and facing problems that will help them into and during adult life. You can help them and you can grow with them. This period can be very enjoyable if you will allow it. As parents, you matter so much, please believe it.

Resources

People

The final decision on how you raise your children will be yours. You weigh up any advantages and disadvantages of what you do with your children and the rules you define. In making these decisions, bear in mind the following:

- In marshalling your resources think broadly and don't underestimate your own energy and skills.
- Remember that good ideas can come from a range of different sources. Some people may be a pain in many ways yet still have good ideas. This can be very true of advice from relatives.
- Come to your own opinion about professional advice. Even people with a string of letters after their name must be able to give sound reasons for what they advise. Remember that it's impossible for experts to know your child as well as you do.

Experts in health, and those who have experience of working with children and families can offer broad, sensible, approaches.

However, it is you who will have to carry out any suggestions and modify them if necessary to work well for your family.

The helping professions

You may find effective help in your work as a parent from a wide range of professions.

Health

This includes:

- your own doctor;
- specialists to whom your doctor could refer you;
- alternative schools of medicine;
- the local child health clinic including health visitors.

Psychological help

This can come from professionals who have different kinds of experience and training. *Psychiatrists* are doctors who have specialised in this particular subject. *Psychologists* have not taken the medical track but have specialised in one or more branch of applied psychology, say, educational or clinical, after taking a degree in psychology. *Therapists* and *counsellors* may have taken a number of different routes to their current position. Whether any of these people can help you depends a lot of their skill. It will also depend on whether you warm to them personally and their approach to helping.

It is reasonable for you to want to know something about the professional who is recommended as a source of help to you or your family. By all means find out:

- the person's experience and qualifications;
- whether he or she has diplomas or certificates in therapy or counselling;
- if they are registered – psychologists should be on the British Psychological Society Register of Chartered Psychologists;

RESOURCES

- what sort of approach the person takes and how this is likely to affect how he or she will work with you and your family;
- how the person will ensure that he or she will keep what you say confidential.

Education

Hopefully your child's teachers will be an effective source of help, information and support to you. As well as class teachers, you may find help from specialist teachers of all kinds and from special units or centres. The availability of different kinds of educational support services varies significantly in different parts of the country. For example, professionals admit, although often off the record, that the chances of having dyslexia acknowledged in your child vary from one authority to another. A lot will depend, therefore, on what is available in your area, whether you can get access and the length of waiting lists.

Organisations

Here is a selection of organisations which may be useful to you at some point. This is in addition to the information we give throughout the book. The organisations do not all operate in anything like the same way. Some are concerned with research, some are established specifically to be supportive of parents. Some are a combination. Many will help with queries as well as being a source of publications, short and long, and of further contacts.

ADVISORY CENTRE FOR EDUCATION   1B Aberdeen Studios, 22–24 Highbury Grove, London N5 2EA. Tel: 071 354 8321. The Centre also offers advice to parents on educational matters within the state system.

ACTION FOR SICK CHILDREN   Argyle House, 29–31 Euston Road, London NW1 2SD. Tel: 071 833 2041. This organisation passes on information about the needs and care of children in hospital.

AFRO-CARIBBEAN EDUCATION RESOURCE CENTRE ACER Centre, Wyvil Road, London SW8 2TJ. Tel: 071 627 2662. The centre has a range of publications, posters and general information.

BRITISH AGENCIES FOR ADOPTION AND FOSTERING 11 Southwark Street, London SE1 1RQ. Tel: 071 407 8800. The above is the central number for BAAF, but they also have regional offices. It is well worth checking on the information and support offered in your own area by your local authority. Some have active adoption and fostering departments with officers who could tell you about local groups and training sessions.

CHILDREN'S LEGAL CENTRE 20 Compton Terrace, London N1 2UN. Tel: 071 359 6251. The Centre runs an advice and information service covering all aspects of law and policy affecting children and young people in England and Wales.

CONTACT A FAMILY 16 Strutton Ground, London SW1P 2HP. Tel: 071 222 2695. This organisation offers support for families who have children with special needs.

COUNCIL FOR DISABLED CHILDREN 8 Wakley Street, London EC1V 7QE. Tel: 071 278 9441. An independent body concerned with children with special needs and their families.

EDUCATION OTHERWISE PO Box 120, Leamington Spa, Warwickshire CV32 7ER. Tel: 0926 886828. A self-help network of parents concerned with educating their children at home. If you send a stamped, self-addressed envelope, they will send you general information.

ENURESIS RESOURCE AND INFORMATION CENTRE (ERIC) 65 St Michael's Hill, Bristol BS2 8DZ. Tel: 0272 26490. ERIC is a national centre offering information and advice to parents and professionals alike on the problem of bed wetting. Most children of 5-11 are successfully dry at night. However, some are not and this can be an embarrassing and difficult issue for children and their parents.

FAMILIES NEED FATHERS 27 Old Gloucester Street, London WC1N 3XX. Tel: 081 295 1956 (general), 081 886 0970 (advice). An organisation for fathers without custody of their children

RESOURCES

after separation or divorce. There are local groups in some areas.

GINGERBREAD   35 Wellington Street, London WC2. Tel: 071 240 0953. Information and support for one-parent families.

HEALTH EDUCATION AUTHORITY   78 New Oxford Street, London WC1 1AH. Tel: 071 631 6930. A national organisation which provides advice and resources relevant to the whole age range. They have a resources centre and are responsive to queries over the telephone about available publications.

ISIS (Independent Schools Information Service)   Headquarters at 56 Buckingham Gate, London SW1E 6AG. Tel: 071 630 8793/ 4. They will give you your nearest local office. ISIS provides information about private schools, consultancy and a placement service. Ask about these services and the cost involved.

MENSA FOUNDATION FOR GIFTED CHILDREN   Mensa House, St John's Square, Wolverhampton WV2 4AH. Tel: 0902 772771. The foundation will give advice about helping gifted children. British Mensa Ltd, at the same address, can be contacted for a test.

NATIONAL CHILDREN'S BUREAU   8 Wakley Street, London EC1V 7QE. Tel: 071 278 9441. This organisation aims to identify and promote the interest of all children and young people and to improve their status in a diverse and multi-racial society. The Early Childhood Unit is part of the NCB. The Unit operates as a national centre for advice and information on current practice, thinking and research.

NATIONAL STEPFAMILY ASSOCIATION   72 Willesden Lane, London NW6 7TA. Tel: 071 372 0844 (office), 071 372 0846 (counselling service). The Association offers information and publications on the subject of stepfamilies and step-parenting. The central counselling number operates weekday afternoons and evenings and will give a list of numbers where confidential help is available. There are local groups and a newsletter.

WORKING GROUP AGAINST RACISM IN CHILDREN'S RESOURCES   460 Wandsworth Road, London SW8 3LX. Tel: 071 627 4594.

WGARCR provides guidelines for a selection of children's books and play materials and books about children, along with a newsletter and a very practical resources list with addresses.

Index

A

abuse, *see* safety, drugs

B

books, using when children have
worries 35
bullying 79, 111–8
fashion bullying 79
helping children who are bullied
113
why children may bully 117

C

clothes and dressing 66–7
arguments over 67
fashion 77–9
communication 43–54
bilingual families 48
body language 43–4

conversation in families 46–9,
53–4
family meetings 26–9
misunderstandings 44–6
speaking up for themselves 97
craft work and creative activities
127–30

D

drugs, abuse of 83–5, 110–1
dyslexia 11, 12

F

families 23–37, 47, 53, 133–5
brother and sister fights 104–7
coping with crisis 23, 24, 34–7
divorce 23, 35–6
family meetings 26–9
planning changes 24–6
spending time together 120

step families 36–37
friends 99–120
    asking friends home 102–4
    communicating house rules to
        104
    fights 104–5
    making friends 99–102
    pressures from 109–11

G

games, playing with children
        85–6, 120–7
    board and card games 125
    physical 120–5

H

hobbies 127–30
household responsibilities 31–2,
        71, 74, 131–2
    getting children to help out 32–3

I

independence, children learning
        63–6
    cooking 63
    dressing 66–7
    first-aid and medicine 65–6
    going out without you 91–6
    gradual process 6, 55–6
    learning by helping out 58–60
    physical care 64
    safety 86–93

J

jobs 81–3
    child care 81–3
    combining parenting 134

L

learning 5–23
    concentration 6–7
    conversation 9, 48–9
    how children learn 6–8, 56,
        58–60, 131, 134
    memorising 12, 13
    specific learning difficulties
        11–12
    study 12–18

M

maths 14, 61
    everyday practice 61–3
    money and maths 62
money 71–80
    earning it 33, 74
    handling it 72–6
    pocket money 33, 73
    saying 'No' to children 76, 80

P

parents and parenting 1–4, 5,
        133–6
    cooperation in two-parent
        families 135

INDEX

emotional wear and tear 11,
108–9
realistic goals 5, 133–6
what only parents can do 2–3, 5
physical
changes 5–11 68–9
dangers to health 83–6, 109–10
games with children 120–6
need for exercise 120–1
puberty 68–9
prejudice 112
children learning 101–2
problems and worries 11, 21,
49–53, 114, 118, 138
helping your children 49–53

R

reading and writing 17, 60–1
everyday learning 60
rules 29–31
for children out alone 91–6
house rules 29–31, 104
making and reviewing rules 31

S

safety 81–98

in the home 86–7
on the road 91–3
personal 89–91
school see also teachers
National Curriculum 15, 19
preparing children for 37–38
sex education 69–70
study, helping children to 11–18
planning work 16–18
workbooks and how to use them
15

T

teachers 3, 38–40, 117, 139
friendly relations with 38, 40
meetings with 39, 40, 117
television 10, 47, 60, 61, 125, 126
tests and exams 18–21
how to help children 19–21
within the National Curriculum
19
test technique 19–20
time, children learning to tell the
62–3
toilet training 65
problems with 5–11s 65